*A*
*Hebrew*
*Chronicle*
*from Prague,*
*c. 1615*

JUDAIC STUDIES SERIES

*Leon J. Weinberger, General Editor*

# A
# *Hebrew Chronicle from Prague,*
## *c. 1615*

*Edited by*
## *Abraham David*

Translated by
Leon J. Weinberger
with
Dena Ordan

THE UNIVERSITY OF ALABAMA PRESS
TUSCALOOSA AND LONDON

Passages translated from *Sefer Ẓemaḥ David* (edited by Mordechai Breuer, Jerusalem, 1983), pp. 132, 133, 137, 139, 141, 143, 145, and 146, are printed here by kind permission of The Magnes Press, The Hebrew University, and the Ben-Zion Dinur Institute for Research in Jewish History of The Hebrew University.

designed by Paula C. Dennis

∞

The paper on which this book is printed meets the minimum requirements of American Standard for Information Science-Permanence of Paper for Printed Library Materials, ANSI Z39.48-1984.

Library of Congress Cataloging-in-Publication Data

Kroniḳah 'Ivrit mi-Prag me-reshit ha-me 'ah ha-17. English.
   A Hebrew chronicle from Prague, c. 1615 / edited by Abraham
David : translated by Leon J. Weinberger with Dena Ordan.
      p.    cm. — (Judaic studies series)
   Includes bibliographical references and index.
   ISBN 0-8173-0596-3
      1. Jews—Czechoslovakia—Prague—History—16th century—Sources.
   2. Jews—Czechoslovakia—Prague—History—17th century—Sources.
   3. Prague (Czechoslovakia)—Ethnic relations—Sources.   I. David,
   Avraham.    II. Weinberger, Leon J.    III. Ordan, Dena.    IV. Title.
   V. Series: Judaic studies series (Unnumbered)
DS135.C96P73713   1993
943.7′ 12004924—dc20                                                    92-26939
                                                                                    CIP
British Library Cataloguing-in-Publication Data available

*To my parents,*
*Hannah and Eliezer David,*
*with love.*

# Contents

# *Preface*

The basis of this work is the manuscript Mic. 3849 in the Jewish Theological Seminary library, New York. In the course of my search for historical sources relating to Jewish life in the Middle Ages, I chanced upon a manuscript of the chronicle during my visit to the seminary in 1978. The chronicle provides valuable evidence of the events and changes in Jewish life in Bohemia and in Prague during the sixteenth and beginning of the seventeenth centuries. I should like to thank Professor Menahem Schmelzer, then librarian, for his permission to publish the manuscript.

Most of the research in this study was done during the time that I was a research associate at the Center for Jewish Studies, Harvard University, in 1981. I should like to thank the chairman of the center, Professor I. Twersky, for his kind hospitality.

This English edition is a translation of the Hebrew edition entitled *Kroniqah 'Ivrit Mi-Prague Me-Reshit Ha-Me'ah Ha-Yud-Zayin (A Hebrew Chronicle from Prague, c. 1615)*. The Hebrew edition was published in 1984 by the Ben-Zion Dinur Center for Research in Jewish History in Jerusalem. I should like to take this opportunity to thank the chairman of the center, Dr. Aaron Kedar, for his permission to publish the English translation.

I would like to express my gratitude to friends and associates for their good help and advice. These include Professor M. Breuer, Mr. Y. Guggenheim, Professor R. Kestenberg-Gladstein, Dr. A. Dagan, Professor Michael Tuck, Professor Ch. Turniansky, Dr. I. J. Yuval, and Mrs. Chava Fränkel-Goldschmidt.

I am deeply indebted to individuals and institutions who helped in the publication of this work. I should like to thank the National Endowment for the Humanities, Washington, D.C., for their translation grant, and Professor L. J. Weinberger, General Editor of the University of Alabama

Press's Judaic Studies Series, for his care in translating the Hebrew text with the help of Ms. Dena Ordan, Jerusalem. My thanks are extended to Mr. Malcolm MacDonald, Director of The University of Alabama Press, to Ms. Nicole Mitchell, Acquisitions Editor, and to the Press staff.

My dearly beloved wife, Chava (née Rechnitz), mother of our five children, has been my unfailing stay and support. I am most fortunate to have her at my side.

Abraham David

# Translators' Note

The chronicle is divided into numbered sections, which are individual entries.

Where the medieval Hebrew text is unclear, Abraham David has provided interpolations within brackets. Glosses also have been supplied by Dr. David, while glosses supplied by the translators are identified as such.

Ellipses printed within brackets indicate that a given passage is untranslatable or that the manuscript is indecipherable.

When the Hebrew usage in the chronicle echoes biblical language, the translators have cited the biblical source in brackets. The translators also have inserted common-era dates.

*A*
*Hebrew*
*Chronicle*
*from Prague,*
*c. 1615*

# Abbreviations

| | |
|---|---|
| *MGWJ* | *Monatsschrift für Geschicte und Wissenschaft des Judentems* |
| *PAAJR* | *Proceedings of the American Academy for Jewish Research* |
| *REJ* | *Revue des études juives* |
| *ZGJD* | *Zeitschrift für die Geschichte der Juden in Deutschland* |

# Introduction

## The Status of Prague in Sixteenth- and Early Seventeenth-Century Bohemia

The establishment of Prague as the capital of the kingdom of Bohemia by Charles IV (king 1346–1378, Holy Roman Emperor 1355–1378) marks a turning point in Prague's history, and the beginning of significant future changes. For a time thereafter the kingdom of Bohemia was under Polish hegemony, becoming part of the Habsburg dominions in 1526 upon the accession of Ferdinand I, brother of Emperor Charles V, to the throne of Bohemia. From 1556 on, when Ferdinand was crowned Holy Roman Emperor as well, the Habsburg emperors and their descendants ruled Bohemia.

The reign of Rudolf II (1576–1612), who made Prague his imperial residence and capital of the empire, and that of his brother Matthias, was the "golden age" of Prague and of Bohemia in general. As capital, Prague acquired the status of a European metropolis, flourishing economically and culturally, attracting officials, diplomats, merchants, and literati from all over Europe. In the process, Prague was transformed into a truly cosmopolitan city. Moreover, although Catholicism was officially protected, both Prague and the kingdom of Bohemia benefited from a policy of religious toleration until the outbreak of the Thirty Years' War in 1618. Indeed, Prague became a center for schismatic Christian sects.[1] Prague's unique position set the tone for its Jewish community as well, mainly from the last third of the sixteenth century.

## The Jewish Community of Prague and Its Environs

The scattered references available are insufficient to form a picture of the medieval Jewish community *(kehillah)* in Prague, let alone of Jewish life in

Bohemia in general. Our sources include fragmentary written records and a few contemporary historical documents.[2] The contribution of the sixteenth-century Jewish chronicler David Gans, himself a resident of Prague, to the record of the Jews of his city and country is minimal; only a handful of references are contained in his historiographical work *Zemah David*.[3]

Recent significant discoveries, although limited in scope, enable us to sketch a partial portrait of the medieval Jewish community in Prague. The extant sources indicate that in the sixteenth century, the Jewish settlement in Prague was concentrated in two separate walled quarters of the Old Town *(Staré Město)*, with the older, larger quarter specifically known as the "Jewish Quarter." During the medieval period, the Jews of Prague developed a dynamic, established *kehillah,* whose activities from 1270 on centered around the Altneuschul.[4]

The reign of Ferdinand I (1526–1562) represents a nadir in Bohemian Jewish history. At the beginning of his reign, Ferdinand protected Bohemian Jewry, even granting them special privileges,[5] but from 1540 on, he imposed restrictions, rescinding the rights he himself had granted. In 1541, because of false accusations of arson brought by the masses against the Jews, Ferdinand issued a decree of expulsion. A year later, convinced of their innocence, the king allowed them to return (*Chronicle,* no. 51). Eighteen years later (1559), he again issued a decree of expulsion, but its execution was delayed several times. The local populace attacked the Jews, burning dozens of houses in the Jewish quarter, and Ferdinand ordered the confiscation of sacred Jewish texts as well. In 1561, Ferdinand promulgated a decree of forced conversion, but few Jews complied, most preferring to take up an itinerant existence (*Chronicle,* nos. 52–54, 56).

Ferdinand's anti-Jewish measures apparently were enacted at the instigation of the Jesuit Counter-Reformation. The Jesuits' deep hatred of the Jews no doubt was influenced by the Jesuits' view that Bohemian Jewry had an encouraging influence on the various Protestant sects and schismatics—the Lutherans, Sabbatarians, and particularly the Anabaptists—whose numbers and prestige seriously threatened the position of the Bohemian Catholic Church (*Chronicle,* no. 30). Ferdinand's son, Maximilian II (king 1563–1576), was more sympathetic to the Jews, rescinding his father's 1559 decree of expulsion (*Chronicle,* no. 56). Similar toleration was extended by Maximilian's son, Rudolf II (king 1576–1612), to various religious sects (*Chronicle,* no. 68).

By the end of the sixteenth century approximately half the Jewish population of Bohemia was concentrated in Prague and its satellite cities. Little is known about Jewish cultural life prior to the end of the sixteenth century; from this point on, however, more extensive information is available because of the prominence of the literary legacy of the MaHaRaL (R. Judah Loew b. Bezalel) in his generation and in future Jewish thought.[6] As mentioned above, Prague was a cosmopolis, the home of enlightened emperors and patrons of the arts, especially from the last quarter of the sixteenth century until the outbreak of the Thirty Years' War. The city attracted Jewish intelligentsia and rabbinic students from various lands, bringing together Talmudists from eastern and western Europe and enlightened Jewish scholars from Germany, Italy, and Spain, with their intellectual baggage from the German and Italian Renaissance. Prague thus developed a coterie of enlightened Jews, who in addition to Torah study devoted a lesser or greater degree of attention to secular studies and the sciences. The leaders of this trend were the MaHaRaL; R. Yom Tov Lipman Heller (author of the *Tosfot Yom Tov*); R. Abraham Horowitz (father of R. Isaiah Horowitz ha-Levi—"ha-Shelah ha-Kadosh"); and the chronicler David Gans, among others. This tendency to delve beyond the narrow confines of halakhah was not universally accepted and created tension within the Prague Jewish community, sections of which opposed secular studies.[7] The intellectual openness of the Prague Jewish community resulted from the removal of social and cultural barriers and constant contact with the Christian environment. This unique atmosphere was made possible by the policy of religious toleration practiced by the emperor-kings succeeding Ferdinand I.[8]

## A Jewish Chronicle from Prague: Content and Character

A Hebrew chronicle of unknown authorship furnishes a new source of information for the late medieval period in Prague and its environs. The manuscript is housed in the library of the Jewish Theological Seminary of America and contains twenty leaves.[9]

The anonymous author's stated goal is to describe briefly the calamities that befell Bohemian Jewry in general, and the Jews of Prague in particular, during the last centuries of the Middle Ages. The author, himself a resident of Prague and a direct witness of events in the late sixteenth and early seventeenth centuries, prefaces his chronicle with the following statement:

"I shall recount the events occurring in the Exile subsequent to the fifth millennium: the expulsions, miracles, and news of other occurrences befalling [the Jews] in Prague and the other lands of our long Exile because of our iniquities, to serve as a token of remembrance for us and our descendants forever" (*Chronicle*, fol. 3r).

His account presents historical events in relatively strict chronological order. It opens with the year 1389, when an accusation of desecration of Hosts led to the death of many Prague Jews (*Chronicle*, no. 1), and concludes with the year 1611, when Prague was the scene of bloody street battles (known as the *Passaukriegsvolkes*) between supporters of Emperor Rudolf II and followers of his brother Matthias. Protective measures instituted by the emperor allowed the Jews to emerge unscathed during these disturbances, and in fact they even participated actively in the defense of the Jewish quarter (*Chronicle*, no. 76).

The author of the chronicle concentrates primarily on events occurring during Ferdinand I's reign, a dark age for Bohemian Jewry. Ferdinand's anti-Jewish measures took various forms: annulment of rights and cancellation of the protective ordinances granted by the king himself upon his ascension to the throne,[10] expulsion edicts issued twice in the space of twenty years (in 1541, and 1561), confiscation of books in 1560, and a decree of forced conversion in 1560–1561 (*Chronicle*, nos. 51–54, 56). In a departure from his usual laconic style, the author provides a relatively lengthy description of the suffering of the Jews of Pösing (near Pressburg, present-day Bratislava) as a result of a blood libel accusation leveled against them in May 1529, in consequence of which several dozen Jews were burned at the stake (*Chronicle*, no. 33).

The author makes no mention of the subsequent return of Jews to Bohemia after Ferdinand's second decree of expulsion, issued in 1561.[11] Indeed, the entire episode of the return of the Jews remains obscure. Although Ferdinand himself was somewhat more tolerant of the remaining Bohemian Jews at the end of his reign, the remigration of the Jews was feasible only during his son Maximilian II's rule, which commenced in September 1563 (*Chronicle*, no. 57).

The chronicle is a fruitful source of information regarding Prague Jewry under Emperor Rudolf II in the early seventeenth century (*Chronicle*, nos. 68–70, 72, 76). Some of the author's disclosures are unique, found in no other extant sources. The author apparently relied directly on his personal experiences as a resident of Prague in his reports of this period, many of which are presented in the first person plural. One example of a singular revelation concerns a scandal that rocked the Jewish community of Prague in 1602—a denunciation that led to the death of a Jewish resident of Prague and brought in its wake the arrest of the Jewish communal leaders, including the renowned luminary, the MaHaRaL (*Chronicle,* nos. 69–70). This episode in the MaHaRaL's life previously was unknown.

The author also devotes space to events affecting Jews outside the borders of Bohemia. He refers to two episodes of messianic expectations that struck a deep chord in western and central Europe. Using general terms, the author alludes first to a messianic movement that originated in Italy in 1502, initiated by an Ashkenazic Jew, R. Asher Lemlein Roitlingen (*Chronicle,* no. 11), and then to a second messianic ferment precipitated by the appearance of David ha-Reuveni and Solomon Molcho in 1523, referring to them and other messengers of redemption at that time without mentioning their names (*Chronicle,* no. 19). The attitude of our author to the messianic phenomenon is difficult to assess precisely. His references to the subject are extremely brief and cryptic, but the very fact that he mentions events predating his own era by two or three generations out of their natural context may indicate that, like his contemporary and fellow citizen of Prague, David Gans, our author evinced a special interest in messianism.[12]

The inclusion of significant highlights and major events in the lives of the Bohemian kings and Habsburg Holy Roman emperors, beginning with Charles I and ending with Rudolf II and his brother Matthias, may reflect the author's view that any attempt to understand anti-Jewish activity must be undertaken in a context broader than a continuous account of specific anti-Semitic incidents. Our author undoubtedly assumed, but does not explicitly state, that increased anti-Jewish activity was the result of the momentous political, social, and religious changes sweeping across Bohemia in the sixteenth and early seventeenth centuries.

Other Jewish historians, too, did not confine themselves solely to Jewish history, but were variously motivated to take an interest in world history.[13] In the course of the sixteenth century, a substantial number of histories were written by Jews, some of whom even devoted entire treatises or chapters of their works to world history. For example, significant data concerning the kings of Spain is provided by the works of Joseph b. Ẓaddik, who resided in pre-expulsion Spain, and Abraham b. Solomon of Torrutiel (Ardutiel), a Spanish exile.[14] Abraham Zacuto devoted the sixth chapter of his *Sefer Yuḥasin (Book of Genealogies)* to a chronological outline of the history of various nations. Even nonhistorical works, like Don Isaac Abravanel's biblical commentary, contain clusters of non-Jewish historical information.[15] Several prominent historians wrote accounts of cities and kings, both ancient and contemporary. The Turkish sultans and the rule of Venice are the subjects of Elijah Capsali's *Seder Eliyahu Zuta (Minor Order of Elijah)* and his chronicle of Venice, respectively.[16] Joseph ha-Kohen's entire treatise *Divrey ha-Yamim le-malkhey Ṣorfat u-malkhey beyt Ottoman ha-Tugar (History of the Kings of France and of the Ottoman Turkish Sultans)* concentrates on the annals of Europe and the Orient. In his *Shalshelet ha-Kabbalah (Chain of Tradition)*, Gedaliah ibn Yaḥya attempts to elucidate the interaction between Jewish history and ancient Greece, the Roman and Byzantine emperors, and Christianity.[17] Our author's contemporary, David Gans, was well aware of the significance of non-Jewish history and devoted the second half of his work *Ẓemaḥ David* to a survey of world history from the birth of mankind to Gans's day (1592).[18]

Similarly, the author of the Prague chronicle relates events in the non-Jewish world. He provides details of the military struggle of the kings of Bohemia and Hungary against the incursions of the Turkish sultan, Suleiman the Magnificent, into Hungary, which ended in their defeat at the decisive battle of Mohács (on the Danube, near the current Yugoslavian border) on 29 August 1526, and the death in battle of Louis II, king of Hungary and Bohemia (*Chronicle*, no. 23). Our author briefly refers to Suleiman's repeated attempts to conquer additional Hungarian and Bohemian territory, mentioning in an aside that the sultan settled "several . . . former Marranos who had returned to Judaism [in Hungary]" (*Chronicle*, no. 22). He is also aware of the sultan's unsuccessful attempts to conquer Vienna in 1530 and 1532, when his armies nearly reached the gates of the Habsburg capital (*Chronicle*, nos. 37, 44). Finally, he alludes to the peace treaty concluded between the antagonists at the beginning of the seventeenth century (*Chronicle*, no. 74).

Our chronicler also tersely recounts Ferdinand I's attempts to recover all of Hungary after being crowned king of Bohemia, and to recover the western parts of Hungary subsequent to the battle of Mohács (*Chronicle*, no. 24). Ferdinand claimed hegemony over Hungary in its entirety, seeking to depose Janos Zapolya, the king installed in Buda, the capital, by the Turkish sultan. Ferdinand's goal was to unite all of Hungary under his crown. To this end he made an unsuccessful attempt to capture Buda in 1530, initially concentrating his troops in nearby Gran [present-day Esztergom —TRANS.] near Buda. However, Ferdinand was forced to withdraw to Pressburg, near Vienna, by Zapolya's army (*Chronicle,* no. 38).

The chronicle twice mentions the sack of Rome (*"Sacco di Roma"*) of 1527, which occurred in the course of the pitched battles fought in northern and central Italy between Charles V of Spain and François I of France. Charles's armies invaded Rome, wreaking havoc and placing Pope Clement VII under arrest (*Chronicle,* nos. 25, 31). Our author stresses the deleterious effects of these events on the Jews of Rome. He also alludes to the reconciliation between the pope and the Spanish king in 1530 that led to Charles's coronation by the pope as Holy Roman Emperor (*Chronicle,* no. 39). In addition to reporting military affairs, the chronicler devotes space to the social and religious tensions that peaked in the first half of the sixteenth century. He is familiar with the 1525 peasant rebellion (*Bauernkrieg*) in Germany (*Chronicle,* no. 20). He briefly relates the birth of the Lutheran Reformation, later prominent in Bohemia, and describes the Anabaptists, whose strongholds were located in Bohemia and Moravia, and their harsh persecution by Ferdinand in 1528 and 1535 (*Chronicle,* nos. 21, 30, 47–48, 73).

Our author gives an extensive eyewitness account of the street disturbances in Prague during the *Passaukriegsvolkes,* the bloody struggle for supremacy between Emperor Rudolf II and his brother Matthias in 1611. Each brother's supporters took to the streets, with Rudolf's Bohemian supporters barricaded on one side of the street and Matthias's Passau supporters on the other. The author notes that the Jewish population of Prague did not suffer during these disturbances, because of the active protection of the emperor (*Chronicle,* no. 76).

In addition to this interest in general history, the chronicler takes note of remarkable natural phenomena: extraordinary climatic conditions—floods (*Chronicle,* nos. 10, 42, 66), small amounts or total absence of snow in winter (no. 27), snow in June (no. 26)—outbreaks of plague (nos. 27, 57), and of changes in the course of the heavenly bodies and their cosmic significance, mentioning solar and lunar eclipses (nos. 36, 49, 50; no. 63), and a rainbow (nos. 35, 40). In one instance, he appends the supplication "May God regard it for good and a blessing, Amen" as his reaction to an unusual astronomical phenomenon (*Chronicle,* no. 64). He ascribes astrological meanings to unusual celestial events and to changes in the laws of nature, thereby expressing his agreement with the accepted contemporary view that the universe was governed by the "rule of stars." This conception regards heavenly signs and deviations from the natural order as harbingers of evil. Similarly, his contemporary and fellow resident of Prague, David Gans, reports noteworthy natural phenomena in his book *Zemaḥ David*.[19] It is likely that both our chronicler and Gans were influenced by their German and Bohemian contemporaries, whose chronicles typically record such natural phenomena.[20]

## The Chronicler's Sources and Method of Writing

Regarding the chronicler's personal history, we can state with certainty only that he resided in Prague at the turn of the seventeenth century. We are completely ignorant of his name or the names of his ancestors, his family status, profession, or cultural background. Nor does the chronicler indicate the date of composition of the chronicle; however, it is likely that it was completed shortly after 1611, the last recorded date. Later entries were made in a different hand, and perhaps were added by the owners of the manuscript between the years 1631 and 1708. The author adheres closely to his stated goal of recording the story of the trials and tribulations of the Bohemian Jewish community, and of Prague Jewry in particular, introducing some general information in the process.

The chronicle is arranged in the form of short entries in chronological order, with the year prominently featured at the beginning of each passage. The author's annalistic method shows similarities to the writing of David Gans, and especially to the method of the Italian Jewish historiographer Joseph ha-Kohen in his *Divrey ha-Yamim* and *Emeq ha-Bakha*. Unlike Gans, however, who completely separated Jewish from general data, our chronicler incorporates general information in its appropriate chronological position, a methodology more like that of Joseph ha-Kohen's *Divrey ha-Yamim*. In ha-Kohen's book, however, the non-Jewish material predominates. Our chronicler's accounts are generally concise and to the point; unlike his fellow historiographers, he saw no need to analyze the underlying causes of events. He writes in simple, colloquial, unembellished Hebrew, reflecting the typical Ashkenazic Hebrew of his milieu, which was influenced by the vernacular (Yiddish) in its pronunciation, vocabulary, and syntax. Occasionally his Hebrew fails to adhere to the proper agreement between singular and plural. In addition, the chronicler utilizes German words and terms where Hebrew lacks specific terminology, but such usage is not confined solely to technical matters.

The data presented by the chronicler receive confirmation from a variety of reliable sources, both Jewish and non-Jewish. A close reading of the chronicle indicates that the author's sources included oral traditions transmitted by family members or city elders, as well as written material. With regard to recorded traditions, the chronicler clearly relied on Hebrew sources like the *pinkas* (minutes book) of the Prague Jewish community, which, although mentioned specifically only once, was evidently more frequently consulted. A large proportion of the chronicler's information, including that pertaining to the Bohemian rulers, was drawn from Hebrew sources. This conclusion is based on the fact that the honorific "may he be exalted" is appended to the names of sixteenth-century monarchs already deceased at the time of the writing of the chronicle, the author not bothering to expunge this typical Hebrew formula despite its irrelevance (*Chronicle,* nos. 24, 25, 28, 32, etc.). Perhaps our chronicler was ignorant of the significance of this abbreviation, in Hebrew י"ר, which he also appended to names of his contemporaries (*Chronicle,* nos. 68, 72, 76, etc.), or else retained it for some unknown reason. It is likely that the author also drew directly from documentary sources or local non-Jewish chronicles.

Several sixteenth-century Hebrew sources contain parallel accounts of events mentioned in the Prague chronicle, with minor differences or complementary material. Comparison of these sources with our chronicle facilitates our understanding of the unfolding of various episodes. Detailed examination reveals that our author made no direct use, even partial, of the extant known sources, not even those accessible to him. He is not familiar with Joseph ha-Kohen's *Divrey ha-Yamim* (Sabbioneta, 1554) and, more surprisingly, makes no use of David Gans's book, *Ẓemaḥ David,* written and published in Prague in 1592. Seventeen events have parallels in *Ẓemaḥ David* (*Chronicle,* nos. 1, 5, 11, 13, 15, 20, 21, 22, 44, 51, 52, 53, 54, 57, 58, 59, 60), but close comparison reveals no dependence. Therefore, we may conclude that the few accounts of events in sixteenth-century Prague reported in *Ẓemaḥ David* and, with minor differences, in our chronicle, are based on a common source. Although there are differences in length and emphasis in the two chronicles, careful reading reveals distinct similarities in the details and the very language used in the recounting of events (*Chronicle,* nos. 51, 52, 54). It is very likely that the now-lost minutes book of the Prague Jewish community was one of the shared Hebrew sources; unfortunately, the *pinkas* apparently perished in the conflagration of the Jewish quarter in the 1670s.

As mentioned above, the chronicler's accounts of various events in sixteenth-century Bohemia and those found in other Hebrew historical sources are mutually complementary. Several examples illustrate this point:

1. The chronicle describes at relatively great length the "blood libel in Pösing" on 1 Sivan 5289 (9 May 1529), and reports that as a result thirty-three Jews were burned at the stake after undergoing cruel torture while under arrest. In conclusion he adds that a commander of the king's army "tried to persecute the Jews . . . based on the confessions of the burned martyrs of Pösing. May God avenge them! But the Holy One, Blessed be He, nullified his [evil] intent" (*Chronicle*, no. 33).

Two additional Hebrew sources partially round out the unfolding of events. R. Joseph of Rosheim, the famous court Jew *(shtadlan)*, mentions this blood libel accusation in his diary, recounting that thirty-six Jews were martyred on 13 Sivan 5289 (21 May 1529). Restricting himself to a brief description of the libel, he treats at length his role in the attempt to free the prisoners, which is only hinted at in the Prague chronicle. R. Joseph of Rosheim notes: "I had to bring copies of old writs of privilege from popes and emperors to the city of Günzberg, where I copied them, with the addition of words of apology, into a booklet, and I forwarded them to the king and his servants, and the justice of our cause became known, and they released the prisoners."[21]

The different sources do not agree on the number of Jews martyred. Our chronicle reports thirty-three, R. Joseph of Rosheim reports thirty-six, and two separate versions of a memorial prayer *(yizkor)* for the martyrs list twenty-four and thirty-one names respectively.

2. The expulsion of Bohemian Jews by Ferdinand I (1541–1542) and their subsequent return (*Chronicle*, no. 51) are mentioned in a number of contemporary Hebrew sources. The following comparison of our chronicle to three of these sources—Joseph ha-Kohen's *Divrey ha-Yamim*,[22] David Gans's *Zemah David*, and R. Joseph of Rosheim's diary—shows how each source treats the account, including or omitting details concerning the events.

| *Chronicle* | *Joseph ha-Kohen* | *David Gans* | *R. Joseph of Rosheim* |
|---|---|---|---|
| [5]301 [1541]–King Ferdinand, may he be exalted, expelled [the Jews] from all the | Then Bohemia sinned against its king and its God, expelling the Jews from Bohemia | There were many large conflagrations throughout Bohemia in [5]301 | In [5]302 [1542], the attribute of justice was outstretched against the [Jews] |

| *Chronicle* | *Joseph ha-Kohen* | *David Gans* | *R. Joseph of Rosheim* |
| --- | --- | --- | --- |
| cities of Bohemia, and here in Prague only ten [Jewish] householders remained. Subsequently, he allowed them to return, with the help of God (no. 51). | and the royal city of Prague in those days because of the wrath of the Lutherans. [The Jews] departed in wagons in the month of Adar 5302 [March 1542], settling in Poland . . . After a time, Ferdinand returned to his throne . . . and spoke well of the Jews, [inviting] them to return, and many returned to their land and birthplace as before. (*Divrey ha-Yamim*, 268r-v; *Emeq ha-Bakha*, pp. 75–76.) | [1541], [set by] an unknown arsonist. The shepherds and the Jews were denounced, the people saying, "You committed this evil." . . . [B]ecause of the accusations of the people, Ferdinand, king of Bohemia, expelled the Jews from the entire kingdom of Bohemia, allowing only ten [Jewish] men to remain in Prague temporarily. But after a short time, within less than a year, the king and the people discovered on whose account this misfortune had come upon them, and realizing that the Jews had been accused falsely, spoke favorably of them . . . and [the Jews] returned to their country and birthplace as before (*Zemah David* 1: 139). | of Bohemia and Prague [like] the fiery serpents bringing severe punishments . . . and a bitter, hasty exile above all. In response to mass appeals, I joined my comrades in misfortune, men of action in the holy community of Prague in their appeal to the king . . . I was finally privileged to witness sons returning to their country, increasing in number and rebuilding what had been destroyed (p. 93). |

The shortest account appears in the Prague chronicle. In keeping with his usual style, the author pays no attention to the underlying circumstances, unlike the other chroniclers. Factually, nothing is missing; moreover, the author of the Prague chronicle adds an important detail not found in two of the other sources, that is, that only "ten [Jewish] householders" remained in Prague. This figure is confirmed in *Zemaḥ David* as well as in general historical sources.

3. Influenced by anti-Jewish celergy, Ferdinand I ordered the confiscation of Jewish books in Prague on 13 March 1560. The books were transported to Vienna and examined by church censors; only later were they returned to their owners (*Chronicle*, no. 54). This incident is recorded in the Prague chronicle, in Joseph ha-Kohen's history, and in David Gans's book.

| *Chronicle* | *Joseph ha-Kohen* | *David Gans* |
|---|---|---|
| [5]320 [1560] – King Ferdinand, may he be exalted, was crowned emperor. He ordered the confiscation of all the [Jewish] books in Prague, and the *ḥazzanim* [cantors] prayed from memory in the synagogue. On Monday the 16th of Sivan [10 June] he sent [the books] to Vienna; their weight was fifty-seven talents. This was the result of accusations by apostates, and only a few books were returned (no. 54). | In the year 5319 [1559] . . . in that year an Ashkenazi apostate, a scoundrel—Judah from Udena was formerly his name in Israel—went and spoke perversely of the Jews. [In consequence] all the holy books in Prague were confiscated. They demanded the prayer books as well, leaving no gleanings, taking [the books] in wagons to the king's court which was situated in Vienna at that time. For it had not been specified what should be done to them and the Jews were greatly afeared, and their hearts were like the heart of a woman in travail. They cried out | [5]319 [1559]. All the holy books in our holy community, Prague, were confiscated by royal permit, in consequence of a false accusation that we prayed for the [non-Jews'] harm. For this reason all the prayer books, along with the remaining books, weighing eighty talents, were sent to Vienna; therefore, even the *ḥazzanim* had to pray from memory in the synagogue, until it became clear and was made known to the king that the accusation was entirely false. All the books were returned. This occurred in the year 5319 [1559] *Zemaḥ David*, 1: 141). |

| *Chronicle* | *Joseph ha-Kohen* | *David Gans* |
|---|---|---|
| | to the Lord, and God made the king kindly disposed to [the Jews], and the books were returned. (*Divrey ha-Yamim,* part 3; Gross ed. pp. 59–60; *Emeq ha-Bakha,* pp. 90–91). | |

In this case, as in others, the account of the Prague chronicle is shorter than the two parallel accounts. Nonetheless, all the pertinent facts found in the other sources are included, with the addition of a new bit of data—the exact date of the shipment to Vienna, 10 June 1560, which matches the date on the royal edict. The other two sources mistakenly assign the events to 1559. The entry in the Prague chronicle shows more affinity to David Gans's account than to Joseph ha-Kohen's. Both our chronicler and Gans stress, in practically identical terms, that the "*hazzanim* prayed from memory," perhaps indicating a common source. However, there are various discrepancies in the two accounts: the year, the weight of the books, and the amount of books returned. The Prague chronicle relates that only "a few books were returned," while David Gans reports that "all the books were returned."

In light of the above, we conclude that the author of the Prague chronicle based his entries on a variety of sources, but *not* on the works of the sixteenth-century Jewish chroniclers. He possessed notes and chronicles unknown to us that also served, at least partially, his contemporary and fellow resident of Prague, David Gans. These anonymous sources are reliable in the main. Examination of the available supplementary material reveals that our author had an accurate grasp of the facts and reported chronological and other details precisely.

## The Manuscript

Manuscript Mic. 3849 came to my attention in the summer of 1978 during a visit to the library of the Jewish Theological Seminary of America. I subsequently examined a microfilm copy of the MS located in the Institute of Microfilmed Hebrew Manuscripts in the Jewish National and University Library at the Hebrew University, Jerusalem, No. 29654. The manuscript, which measures 15 × 20 cm, contains twenty leaves in various seventeenth-century Ashkenazic scripts. The bulk of the manuscript is the chronicle of Prague, which concludes with the year 1611 and was transcribed by two, or perhaps three, copyists. The second handwriting begins where the first leaves off, at no. 66, with the year 1598. Entries relating to the years 1631–1693 (fols. 16v, 20r–v) were added by one or another of the owners of the manuscript. Many words are indecipherable either because they were inked out or were hidden by pieces of paper pasted over the original words.

A short list of twenty-two calamities (murder, blood libel, forced conversion, and expulsion) is appended to the beginning of the manuscript. It is a memorial of religious persecutions and calamities suffered by European Jewry, particularly German Jewry, from the persecutions of 1096 until the expulsion of the Jews from Regensburg in 1519 (the chronicle gives 1520 as the date of the latter). This list, which appears here as List A, is recorded in a handwriting different from those in the chronicle, and includes well-known and even famous events, along with others unknown from any other Hebrew source, although familiar from general historical sources.

The Prague chronicle and this list were definitely not authored by the same person. This conclusion is based not only on disparities in handwriting, but also on differences in the accounts of the one event appearing in both documents. Each document refers to the decree of Mark Brandenburg in 1510. The description in List A, although brief, contains details not included in the Prague chronicle, while the Prague text includes a more precise date.

| *Chronicle* | *List A* |
|---|---|
| [5]270 [1510]–On the 12th of Av [19 July] there was the decree of Mark due to our iniquities. May God avenge them! (no. 14) | [5]270 [1510]. There was a decree in the realm of Markgraf Brandenburg, kown as Markgraf Joachim (par. 21). |

List A is not original, but is based on one or more chronological lists circulating among German Jewry in the sixteenth century. This conclusion is based upon the almost exact linguistic identity of various details in List A with those found in another list, which we shall call List B, that enumerates calamities befalling German Jewry in different locales during the final decade of the fifteenth century and the first quarter of the sixteenth century. This list is appended anonymously, and out of its proper chronological order, to a manuscript of R. Isaac of Corbeil's *Amudey Golah*.[23] The author of the list mentions several family members: his father, "Eliezer b. R. Nathan Zack, of blessed memory, called Lieberman" (d. 1530), his youngest daughter "Kroinlein" born in Adar I 5307 (January/ February 1547), and his mother "Gittlen" who died in 5278 [1518] and was buried at Donauwörth. The writer, who resided in Donauwörth until the expulsion of the Jews in 5278 [1518], refers to additional members of his family as well.

Two examples will serve as a basis for comparison.

### Example 1

| *List A* | *List B* |
|---|---|
| 249 in the sixth millennium [1489]. The Markgraf and the archbishop of Würzburg expelled their Jews (fol. 2r). | In the year [5]249 [1489] the prince Markgraf and the archbishop of Würzburg expelled their Jews (fol. 353r). |

### Example 2

| *List A* | *List B* |
|---|---|
| [5]258 [1498]. There was a decree of forced conversion in the lands of Portugal, with most [Jews], young and old, forced to convert from Judaism, mingling [with the non-Jews] (fol. 2r). | At the beginning of the year [5]248 [1498] rumors came of a forced conversion in the land of Portugal. All, young and old, were forced to convert from Judaism, and to mingle [among the non-Jews] (fol. 353r). |

The author of List B places greater emphasis on the damage incurred by individuals and the community at large, over and above the actual fact of expulsion. For example, he states, "The archbishop appropriated the synagogue and the cemetery, and sold their houses" (fol. 353r).

\* \* \*

Sixteenth-century Jewish historiography is devoted largely to descriptions of varying length of the decrees and calamities that befell various Jewish communities. Some of these works are restricted to a limited temporal and geographical span, while others treat extensive areas over a period of centuries.

We have presented in this book three examples of such chronicles, which combine to create a concise picture of the edicts and persecutions affecting western and central European Jewry in the waning days of the medieval era.

# Notes

1. The political, social, and cultural changes affecting Bohemia at the close of the medieval era have been studied extensively. For an up-to-date summary of the subject, see K. Bosl, *Handbuch der Geschichte der böhmischen Länder*, 2 vols. (Stuttgart, 1967–74).

2. Royal records concerning the Jews were compiled by G. Bondy and F. Dworsky, *Zur Geschichte der Juden in Böhmen, Mähren und Schlesien*, 2 vols. (Prague, 1906). Other royal documents concerning Bohemian Jewry are found in scholarly studies cited below. The Jewish chroniclers, like Joseph ha-Kohen, David Gans, and R. Joseph of Rosheim (see below), paid scant attention to the affairs of the medieval Bohemian Jewish community.

3. David Gans's historiographical methods, as presented by M. Breuer in his edition of *Sefer Ẓemaḥ David* (Jerusalem, 1983), and in his studies of Gans and his works, do not provide an adequate explanation for the strange lack of information regarding his city and country in his lifetime and the preceding generations.

4. On communal life in medieval Prague, see the summary in S. Steinherz, ed., *Die Juden in Prag: Bilder aus ihrer tausendjährigen Geschichte* (Prague, 1927); O. Muneles, *Prague Ghetto in the Renaissance Period* (Prague, 1965); and below.

5. See S. Steinherz, "The Expulsion of the Jews from Bohemia in 1541" (Hebrew), *Zion* 15 (1950): 71–74.

6. Many monographs have been written on the MaHaRaL and his thought. See, for example, A. Gottesdiener, "Ha-Ari She-be-Ḥakhmey Prag," in *Azkarah le-nishmat . . . Ha-Rav Kook, Qoveṣ Torani Madai* 3 (1937): 253–430; A. F. Kleinberger, *The Educational Theory of the Maharal of Prague* (Hebrew) (Jerusalem, 1962); A. Neher, *Le puits de l'Exil: La théologie dialectique du Maharal de Prague* (Paris, 1966).

7. See M. Breuer, "R. David Gans, Author of the Chronicle *Ẓemaḥ David*" (Hebrew), *Bar Ilan* 11 (1973): 97–103; Breuer, *Ẓemaḥ David* 1: iv–v.

8. See Breuer, "R. David Gans," 103–4.

9. Ms. Mic. 3849, Jewish Theological Seminary of America. I made an initial public presentation of the contents of this chronicle at the Eighth World Congress of Jewish Studies in the summer of 1981. The presentation appeared in the *Proceedings* of that Congress, vol. 2 (Hebrew; Jerusalem, 1982), 63–70.

10. On 21 March 1527, Ferdinand granted a protective charter to Bohemian

Jewry, similar to those of his predecessors. See Bondy and Dworsky, *Zur Geschichte der Juden,* 254–55; Steinherz, "Expulsion of the Jews," 71–74.

11. David Gans makes no reference to the return of the Jews under Maximilian II in his *Ẓemaḥ David.* However, the anonymous proofreader of the book *Emeq ha-Bakha* clearly hints at this course of events, writing: "His sons were merciful kings, favorably inclined towards the Jews, saying to them, 'have no fear, dwell in the land and acquire holdings in it. You will be men, dwelling safely in your land.'" See Joseph ha-Kohen, *Emeq ha-Bakha,* ed. K. Almbladh (Uppsala, 1981), 98.

12. On David Gans, see B. Z. Degani, "The Structure of World History and the Redemption of Israel in R. David Gans's *Ẓemaḥ David*" (Hebrew), *Zion* 45 (1980): 196–200. See also Breuer, *Ẓemaḥ David,* xxi–xxii.

13. See H. H. Ben-Sasson, "Trends in Medieval Jewish Chronography" (Hebrew) in *Historians and Historical Schools* (Hebrew; Jerusalem, 1962), 32–34; H. Y. Yerushalmi, "Clio and the Jews: Reflections on Jewish Historiography in the Sixteenth Century," *PAAJR (Jubilee Volume)* 46–47 (1979–80): 624–25.

14. Concerning their writings, see A. David, ed., *Two Chronicles from the Generation of the Spanish Exile* (Hebrew) (Jerusalem, 1979), v–xvi.

15. See B. Netanyahu, *Don Isaac Abravanel* (Philadelphia, 1972), 130–49.

16. The Venice Chronicle was published by N. Porges, *REJ* 79 (1924): 28–60, and recently in his edition of the historiographical work *Seder Eliyahu Zuta* 2 (Jerusalem, 1977), 215–327.

17. See A. David, "The Historiographical Work of Gedaliah ibn Yaḥya, Author of *Shalshelet ha-Kabbalah*" (Hebrew; Ph.D. diss., Hebrew University, Jerusalem, 1976), 23–62.

18. See Degani, "Structure of World History," 173ff.; Breuer, *Ẓemaḥ David,* xvi–xxi.

19. See Breuer, "R. David Gans," 109–13; idem, *Ẓemaḥ David,* viii–ix.

20. I. Sedinova, "Czech History as Reflected in the Historical Work by David Gans," *Judaica Bohemiae* 8 (1972): 80–81.

21. See "Rabbi Joselmann de Rosheim: Diary" (French), ed. J. Kracauer, *REJ* 16 (1888): 90.

22. Joseph ha-Kohen, *Divrey ha-Yamim le-malkhey Ṣorfat u-malkhey beyt Ottoman ha-Tugar* (2 vols., Sabbioneta, 1554; vol. 3, ed. D. A. Gross, Jerusalem, 1955).

23. The original is in the British Library, MS. 514 (Add. 18684); a copy is located at the Institute of Microfilmed Hebrew Manuscripts (Jerusalem), no. 4978, fols. 352v–353r.

*The Hebrew Chronicle*

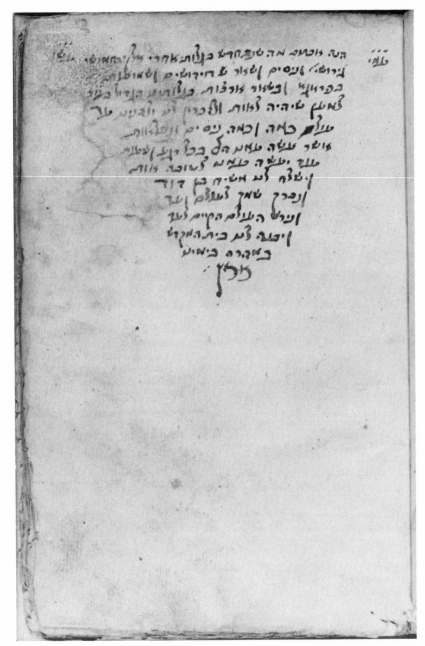

A page from the *Hebrew Chronicle*. The manuscript is housed at the Jewish Theological Seminary of America in New York. (Photograph by Suzanne Kaufman; reproduced courtesy of the Library of the Jewish Theological Seminary of America.)

## [Fol. 3r]

I shall recount the events occurring in the Exile subsequent to the fifth millennium: the expulsions, miracles, and news of other occurrences befalling [the Jews] in Prague and the other lands of our long exile because of our iniquities,** to serve as a token of remembrance for us and our descendants forever. May God who renders miracles daily, even hourly, grant us a favorable sign, and send the Messiah, son of David, that we may praise Your name forever, and inherit the everlasting world. May the Temple be rebuilt speedily in our day. Amen.

\* The page opens with an abbreviation of this verse, Psalms 121:2— ʿmy ʿshv—with each half appearing on opposite margins.

\*\* The formula be- ʿavvonotaynu ha-rabim appears in abbreviation throughout the chronicle, but does not indicate a literal belief in a causal relationship between sin and punishment. Israel's suffering in exile because of her sins absolves God from blame. —TRANS.

## [Fol. 4r]

[1]* In the 149th year of the sixth millennium, on the day after Passover, *Isru Ḥag* [18 April 1389], the decree of Yanek was issued in Prague, due to our iniquities.

\* Bracketed numbers refer to paragraphs in the manuscript. The historical notes at the base of each page refer to these numbered paragraphs. —TRANS.

**decree** The Hebrew *gezeyrah* has been translated throughout as *decree*. It is used in the broad sense of persecution, something allotted by fate, an official edict, or all of the above. —TRANS.

---

1. On the last day of Passover 5149 (18 April 1389) many Prague Jews met their death, the result of an accusation of Host desecration. According to a non-Jewish source, approximately 3,000 Jews were burned to death or otherwise killed. See G. Bondy and F. Dworsky, *Zur Geschichte der Juden* 1: 82–84, no. 171. In commemoration of this tragic event, R. Avigdor Kara, one of the leading Jewish scholars in Prague at the time, composed the elegy "Et Kol ha-Telaah asher Mezaatnu" ("All the Hardships That Have Befallen Us"); cf. S. Bernfeld, *Sefer ha-Demaot (The Book of Tears)* (Berlin, 1924) 2: 159–64. This event is also mentioned in Joseph ha-Kohen's *Divrey ha-Yamim,* fols. 88v–89r (translated into English by C. H. F. Bialloblotzky, *The Chronicles of Rabbi Joseph ben Joshua ben Meir the Sphardi* [London, 1835] 1: 254–55, par.

**fifth millennium** should read sixth.

**Sarsig** unclear word; see historical notes.

**5231** Most of the dates in the chronicle appear in shortened form, with no indication of the millennium. For the sake of clarity the millennium has been added throughout the translation of the text without square brackets. —TRANS.

[2]  In the 225th year of the fifth millennium [1465], due to our iniquities, a decree was issued in Prague.

[3]  209 in the sixth millennium [1449], on a Monday, a d[ecree] against the Jews of Prague, because of our iniquities.

[4]  5231 [1471] – On Saturday, the 2nd of Nisan [24 March], King Sarsig died.

[5]  5231 [1471] – On the 1st of Elul [18 August] the Polish king came to Prague.

337); Joseph ha-Kohen, *Emeq ha-Bakha,* 50 (translated into English by H. S. May, *The Vale of Tears* [The Hague, 1971], 54); Gedaliah ibn Yahya, *Shalshelet ha-Kabbalah (Chain of Tradition),* fol. 114r–v. Cf. David, "The Historiographical Work of Gedaliah ibn Yahya," 127; David Gans, *Zemah David* 1: 132–33. See also Degani, "Structure of World History," 193–94.

In E. Zimmer's edition of the *Wormser Minhagbuch des R. Jousep (Juspa) Schammes* (Jerusalem, 1988) 1: 96–97, par. 89, we find that in Worms a memorial prayer was recited on the eighth day of Passover in memory of those who died in the Prague decree, worded as follows: "May God remember the souls of the martyrs of Prague, who died on this day in sanctification of the Name, among the immortal souls of Abraham, Isaac, Jacob, Sarah, Rebekah, Rachel, and Leah. May they be rewarded with eternal life, and may their souls be bound up in the bond of life, etc." Our chronicle refers to this event as the decree of Yanek; however, the identity of the author of the decree is unknown. Regarding this decree see also J. Kaufman, *R. Yom Tov Lipmann Muelhausen* (Hebrew; New York, 1927), 19, as well as F. Talmage's introduction in *Sefer Hanizzahon: Yom Tov Lipmann Muelhausen* (Hebrew; Jerusalem, 1983), x.

2.  No other known documentation exists for this Prague decree of 1465.
3.  No other known documentation exists for this Prague decree of 1449.
4.  The name "Sarsig" is unknown. Perhaps it refers to the Bohemian king George von Podiebrad (d. 22 March 1471). See K. Bosl, *Handbuch,* 2: 57–61. The Hebrew date does not coincide with 22 March 1471, which fell on the 29th of Adar II. Perhaps the chronicler is referring to the date of the king's burial, which took place two days later.
5.  The reference is to Wladislaw II, the son of Casimir IV, the Polish monarch who was crowned as king of Bohemia on 22 August 1471 and reigned until 1516. He also ruled Hungary from 1490. See Bosl, *Handbuch* 2: 103ff. There is a discrepancy between the dates. The 1st of Elul 5231 corresponds to 18 August 1471, which was not the date

[6]   5244 [1483] – On Simḥat Torah [23 September], many Jews here [Prague] were robbed.

[7]   5254 [1494] – Because of our iniquities, the Jews were expelled from the land of Russia.

[8]   5258 [1498] – On the Sabbath, the 4th of Sivan [25 May], because of our iniquities, the k[ehillah] of Trebitsch was burned, thus sanctifying the Divine name. May God avenge them!

[9]   5258 [1497/8] – Our esteemed rabbi and teacher, R. Meir Pfefferkorn, recited the Talmudic tractate *Bava Kamma* from memory, and gave daily lessons in halakhah, beginning after Hanukkah [November or December 1497] and finishing on the 28th of Adar II [22 March 1498] in the holy community of Ofen. May his soul be bound up in the bond of everlasting life.

**here [Prague]** The owner of the manuscript pasted a piece of paper with the word "Prague" over the word "here."

**Trebitsch** or Trebic, in Moravia.
**kehillah** community.

**Ofen** Budapest.

---

of the coronation. The Hebrew date may refer to the king's arrival in Prague four days prior to the ceremony. The coronation is also reported in *Ẓemaḥ David* 2: 374.

6.   Attacks on Prague Jewry on this date, 24 September 1483, are recorded in additional sources. Cf. Bondy and Dworsky, *Zur Geschichte der Juden*, 163–64, no. 279. Another contemporary reference to looting and pillaging of the Jewish community by local rabble is found in a Bohemian chronicle. See J. Polak-Rokycana, "Die Geschichte der Juden in Böhmen in den alten böhmischen Jahrbüchern," *Zeitschrift für die Geschichte der Juden in der Tschechoslowakei* 2 (1931): 175–76.

7.   Perhaps this entry refers to the expulsion of the Jews from Lithuania in 1495 in reaction to Jewish influence on the "Judaizing sects" in eastern Europe. See S. Ettinger, "Jewish Influence on the Religious Ferment in Eastern Europe at the End of the Fifteenth Century" (Hebrew), *Yitzhak F. Baer Jubilee Volume* (Jerusalem, 1960), 228–47.

8.   Trebitsch is located in Moravia. No other known documentation exists for this event.

9.   R. Meir Pfefferkorn was a relative and the teacher of the well-known apostate Johannes Pfefferkorn. A student of R. Joseph Colon, the leading Italian rabbi of the latter half of the fifteenth century, R. Meir Pfefferkorn was one of the major Prague scholars in the late fifteenth century, and a personal friend of R. Jacob Pollack, a prominent Prague judge *(dayyan)*. See H. Graetz, *History of the Jews* (Philadelphia, 1956) 4: 418. We also have R. Meir's autograph as presiding judge on a document

[10]  5261 [1501] – On Rosh Ḥodesh Elul [15 August], the waters prevailed [Gen. 7:19–20], making our synagogue here in Prague unusable.

[11]  5262 [1502] – News came of the messianic king, causing massive repentance among the many communities of Israel.

authorizing an agent to deliver a bill of divorce, dated the 11th day of the month of Kislev, 5258, signed Meir ben Menahem Pfefferkorn of blessed memory (MS. New York, Jewish Theological Seminary Rab. 623, Mic. 6456 [Acc. 0811]; [Institute of Microfilmed Hebrew Manuscripts no. 39313], fols. 106v–107r. My thanks to A. Reiner for drawing my attention to this document.) Perhaps R. Meir's son was Yonah Poriah b. R. Meir Pfefferkorn, one of the wealthier Prague Jews, whose gravestone (1586) was copied by K. Lieben, *Gal-ed* (Hebrew; Prague, 1856), 70, no. 137.

10. ———

11. This entry alludes to the activity of the false arouser of messianic hopes, R. Asher Lemlein Roitlingen Ashkenazi, who lived in the district of Venice, and successfully spread his messianic tidings and calls for repentance to a broad following. The reverberations of this movement are reflected in both Jewish and non-Jewish sources. See Joseph ha-Kohen, *Divrey ha-Yamim*, fol. 123v (Bialloblotzky, *Chronicles of Rabbi Joseph* 1: 354, par. 475); idem, *Emeq ha-Bakha*, 67–68 (May, *Vale of Tears*, 73–74); Abraham Farissol, *Magen Abraham (Shield of Abraham)*, sections of which were published by S. Löwinger, "Recherches sur l'oeuvre apologétique d'Abraham Farissol," *REJ* 105 (1940): 35ff; Gedaliah ibn Yaḥya, *Shalshelet ha-Kabbalah (Chain of Tradition)*, fol. 45r–v; and David Gans, *Ẓemaḥ David* 1: 137. See also the works of two non-Jews: Sebastian Münster—see A. Z. Aescoly, *Jewish Messianic Movements* (Hebrew; Jerusalem, 1956), 311; and the apostate Johannes Isak—see A. Marx, "Le faux Messie Ascher Lemlein," *REJ* 61 (1911): 135–36.

Abraham Farissol, Joseph ha-Kohen, and Gedaliah ibn Yaḥya stressed the element of repentance associated with the coming of the Messiah, only alluded to in the Prague chronicle, as well as the role played by R. Asher Lemlein, not mentioned by name in our chronicle, in spreading the messianic tidings. Two versions exist regarding the date of his appearance. Gedaliah ibn Yaḥya, David Gans, and the above-mentioned apostate, Johannes Isak, cite 1500 as the date of Lemlein's appearance, while our chronicle, Abraham Farissol, Sebastian Münster, and apparently Joseph ha-Kohen as well, cite 1502. (Although Joseph ha-Kohen does not date Lemlein's appearance in *Divrey ha-Yamim*, the account in *Emeq ha-Bakha* directly follows an oblique reference to 1502. Regarding Lemlein, Joseph ha-Kohen states: "At that time.") The logical conclusion is that this messianic ferment with its calls for repentance lasted for two years, from 1500 to 1502. Gedaliah ibn Yaḥya notes Lemlein's initial appearance: "In 5260 [1500] a Jew appeared," and Abraham Farissol the movement's end: "In the end everything was futile and pursuit of wind. I witnessed these events in 5262 [1502]." See David, "Historiographical Work of Gedaliah ibn Yaḥya," 186–87.

This movement had widespread influence among the Jewish communities of west-

[12]  5266 [1505] – On Friday, the 16th of Tevet
      [12 December], because of our iniquities,
      there was a decree in Budweis. May God
      avenge them!

**Budweis**  or Budějovice,
in Bohemia.

[13]  5269 [1509] – On the Sabbath of the por-
      tion of *Sheqalim*, His Majesty King Lud-
      wig came from Hungary with his father,
      [King] Wladislaw. He was three years old
      on the 27th of Adar I [17 February] and was
      crowned in Prague on Sunday, the 19th of
      Adar II [11 March].

**Sheqalim**  the Scripture
reading from Exod. 30:11–
16 for the Sabbath before
the new moon of Adar.

---

ern and central Europe. David Gans provides a telling illustration of the agitation
among German Jewry. He writes: "R. Lemlein announced the coming of the Messiah
[and] my master and teacher, my grandfather, Seligmann Gans of blessed memory,
smashed the special oven [used only] for the baking of matzah, based on [R. Asher's]
promise that next year he would bake the unleavened bread in the Holy Land. I
myself, the writer, heard from my venerable teacher R. Eliezer Trèves, the rabbi of the
holy community of Frankfurt, that this was no empty gesture, for [R. Asher] gave signs,
and he said that perhaps our sins delayed the coming of the Messiah." New material
concerning R. Asher Lemlein's life, kabbalistic thought, and revelations has been
published by E. Kupfer, "The Revelations of R. Asher b. R. Meir called Lemlein
Roitlingen" (Hebrew), *Kobez al Yad* 8 (1975): 385–423. Kupfer cites this entry from
the Prague chronicle at the conclusion of his article, p. 423.

12.  On the blood libel accusation against the Jews following the murder of a Christian
     child in the Bohemian city of České Budějovice (Budweis), which resulted in Jewish
     deaths there at the end of 1505, see A. Stein, *Die Geschichte der Juden in Böhmen*
     (Brünn, 1904), 34–37. Prague Jewish Museum MS. no. 24 contains a synagogue
     pamphlet with a memorial prayer *(yizkor)* devoted to the memory of the "souls of the
     sainted martyrs of Budweis . . . who withstood temptation and sacrificed themselves
     for the sanctification of God's awesome Name, dying as martyrs in a public execution
     by burning." The text enumerates the names of seven of the town's Jews. A facsimile of
     this text was published by A. Sheiber, "The Martyrs of Phising" (Hebrew), *Aresheth* 6
     (1980): 229. The old *pinkas* of the Kraków Jewish burial society listed more than two
     hundred Jews martyred as a result of this blood libel. See N. Sokolow, *Ha-Asif* 6
     (1894): 133. Unfortunately, the whereabouts of this important *pinkas* is unknown. See
     also List B, par. c: "In 5265 [1505] the Jews of Budweis sanctified the Name of God,
     Blessed be He."

13.  The monarch is Ludwig (Louis) II, king of Hungary and Bohemia, son of Wladislaw
     (Vladislaus) II. Born 1 July 1506, he was crowned king of Hungary in 1508 and of
     Bohemia in 1509. In actuality he ruled from 1516 (see *Chronicle*, no. 15) until 29
     August 1526 when killed at the battle of Mohács, where the Hungarian forces were
     defeated decisively by the Ottoman Turks. On Louis II, see Bosl, *Handbuch* 2: 108–
     11. His coronation in Prague is also reported in *Zemah David* 2: 381–82.

[14]  5270 [1510] – On the 12th of Av [19 July],
there was the decree of Mark [Branden-
burg] due to our iniquities. May God
avenge them!

## [Fol. 4v]

[15]  5276 [1516] – On the 5th of Nisan [8
March], King Wladislaw died in Hungary.

[16]  5277 [1516] – On the 12th of Kislev [7 No-
vember], there was a fire in the Prague
Judenstraße; three houses were burned.

**Judenstraße**   the Jewish
quarter.

[17]  5282 [1522] – On Friday, the eve of Rosh
Ḥodesh Nisan [28 March], King Ludwig
arrived in Prague.

[18]  5283 [1523] – It rained from the 29th of
Sivan [12 June] until the 24th of Tammuz
[7 July]. And the Turks gathered, and conquered all of the land of Egypt, capturing
their leader, known in German as the sul-

---

14. The persecution of the Jews of Berlin, part of the Mark of Brandenburg, resulted in the
death of thirty-eight Jews as attested to by R. Joseph of Rosheim: "In the year [5]270
. . . in that year trouble struck the realm of Mark and thirty-eight pure souls were
burned . . . in the city of Berlin. May their souls be bound up in the bond of
everlasting life." See Kracauer, "Rabbi Joselmann de Rosheim," 88 n. 5, 92–93 n. 22.
On 19 July 1510, which corresponds to the Hebrew date given in the Prague
chronicle, these Jews were executed as the result of an accusation of Host desecration
and blood libel. See Graetz, *History of the Jews* 4: 439–40; W. Heise, *Die Juden in
der Mark Brandenburg bis zum Jahre 1571* (Berlin, 1932), 210–27. The names of the
martyrs are found in the memorial book of the Münden Jewish community. See L.
Löwenstein, "Memorbücher," *ZGJD* 1 (1887): 196–97; thirty-five names appear in
this list. This example of martyrdom is also noted in List A, par. 21.
15. His death in March 1516 is also noted by David Gans, *Ẓemaḥ David*, 384. See Bosl,
*Handbuch* 2: 105–9.
16. A description of the fire in the Prague Judenstraße is also found in a Bohemian
chronicle. Cf. Polak-Rokycana, "Die Geschichte der Juden in Böhmen," 81.
17. ——
18. There are inaccuracies in this account. Egypt was conquered by the Ottoman Turks in
early 1517. Perhaps the chronicler confused the conquest of Egypt in 1517 with the

tan of Egypt, and taking him to their land
[Turkey].

[19]  5283 [1523] – News of saviors from beyond
the Sambatyon River spread among all the
lands, in addition to other messianic expectations.

[20]  5285 [1525] – The peasants in the land of
Germany united [in revolt], refusing to pay
taxes to their overlords, and the lords
feared them. [The peasants] looted various
places and expelled many rulers. Their rebellion lasted nearly a year, until [the
leaders] in Germany fought them, killing
many.

---

suppression of the Ahmad Pasha rebellion by Suleiman the Magnificent in 1524,
when Egyptian Jewry was in danger of extermination. See Elijah Capsali, *Seder Eliyahu
Zuta (Minor Order of Elijah)* (Jerusalem, 1977) 2: 147–201; A. David, "The Termina-
tion of the Office of *Nagid* in Egypt and Biographical Data Concerning the Life of
Abraham Castro" (Hebrew), *Tarbiz* 41 (1972): 332–33.

19.  This entry refers to the inception of the messianic movements associated with David
ha-Reuveni and Solomon Molcho. During this period, various messianic precursors
and bearers of apocalyptic tidings were active. For example, R. Abraham ha-Levi ha-
Sefaradi sent letters and notices of the coming redemption from Jerusalem at the end of
the second and third decades of the sixteenth century. See David ha-Reuveni, *Sippur*,
ed. A. Z. Aescoly (Hebrew, Jerusalem, 1940); Aescoly, *Jewish Messianic Movements*
(Jerusalem, 1956), 326–414; G. Scholem and M. Beit-Aryeh, *Introduction to the
facsimile edition of the treatise "Sefer Meshare Qitrin" of Abraham b. Eliezer Ha-Levi*
(Hebrew; Jerusalem, 1977): D. Tamar, "Messianic Expectations in Italy for the Year
1575" (Hebrew), *Sefunot* 2 (1958): 61–88 (reprinted in *Studies in the History of
the Jewish People in Erez Israel and in Italy* [Hebrew; Jerusalem, 1970], 11–83);
A. David, "A Letter from Jerusalem from the Early Ottoman Period in Eretz-Yisrael"
(Hebrew), in A. Cohen, ed., *Jerusalem in the Early Ottoman Period* (Jerusalem, 1979),
39–60; J. Hacker, "A New Letter on the Messianic Fervor in Eretz Israel and the
Diaspora in the Early 16th Century" (Hebrew), *Shalem* 2 (1976): 355–60.

20.  This entry refers to the German *Bauernkrieg* (peasant revolt) of 1525. See G. Franz,
*Der deutsche Bauernkrieg* (Darmstadt, 1975). A short description of the peasant
uprising appears in *Zemaḥ David* 2: 387. For a summary of the anti-Jewish implica-
tions of the peasant uprising, see S. W. Baron, *A Social and Religious History of the
Jews* (Philadelphia, 1969) 13: 268–69, 449–50, and List B, par. 7.

**priests** The author uses the Yiddish word *galkhes.* **Fridays** *she'at hasheqer,* literally "the hour of falsehood" [the crucifixion. —TRANS.]

[21] 5285 [1525] – A priest named Martinus Luther created turmoil in the Catholic religion, deriding and repudiating its customs. At the same time, the peasants rose up against the priests, seeking to expel them, and the priests were much afraid. There were others among the clergy who sympathized with Luther, despising their dogmas. Subsequently they agreed that priests could marry, that meat could be eaten on Fridays, that certain holy days should be abolished, that the Eucharist is false, and that

21.   The author displays a neutral attitude toward Martin Luther, expressing neither sympathy nor derision for the Lutheran Reformation. Other Jewish leaders reacted positively to this movement, viewing any phenomenon weakening the Catholic Church as auspicious for the Jews. Cf. R. Lewin, *Luthers Stellung zu den Juden* (Berlin, 1911); H. H. Ben-Sasson, "The Reformation in Contemporary Jewish Eyes," *The Israel Academy of Sciences and Humanities, Proceedings* 4 (1970): 239–326. For a summary of research regarding Luther's attitude toward the Jews, see Baron, *Social and Religious History* 13: 216–19, 421–29.

   The chronicler mentions several canonical principles specifically repudiated by the Lutherans and the followers of Zwingli (between whom he made no distinction):

   1. "They agreed that priests could marry": revocation of the prohibition forbidding priests and monks to marry.
   2. "Meat could be eaten on Fridays" (literally "the hour of falsehood," the crucifixion): The Lutherans nullified the prohibition against the consumption of meat on Fridays, the day of the crucifixion, following the reform instituted by Zwingli in 1522.
   3. "Certain holy days be abolished": the abolition of various holy days established by the Catholic Church, especially saints' days and practices associated with the reliquary cult.
   4. "The Eucharist is false": The sacrament of the Eucharist, also known as the Lord's Supper, was abolished by Zwingli and his camp. Luther and his followers maintained the practice of the Eucharist; however, they endowed this sacrament with a more symbolic meaning.
   5. "The crucifix has no substance": the elimination of the cult of crucifixes in the church.

   The import of the concluding sentence of this section is unclear.

## [Fol. 5r]

crucifixes have no substance. They wanted to cancel [ . . . ] as well, and [ . . * . . ].

[22] 5285 [1525] – The Turks gathered large forces, conquering that country [Hungary] as well, killing several thousands. [The Sultan] settled several householders [in Hungary], former Marranos who had returned to Judaism.

[23] 5286 [1526] – Thousands of Turks took the field to do battle against Hungary, killing eighty thousand of the [enemy] vanguard, capturing all of Hungary, and killing its king.

[ . . * . . ]   The meaning of this phrase is unclear.

**large forces**   A doubtful reading of the Hebrew; it was deciphered after removal of a piece of paper pasted over the text.

---

22.  The chronicler recounts the expansionist campaigns of the Ottoman sultan Suleiman the Magnificent (sultan 1520–1566), including his successful invasion of Hungary at the beginning of 1526. See R. B. Merriman, *Suleiman the Magnificent* (Cambridge, Mass., 1944), 76ff. These events are recorded in *Zemaḥ David* 2: 388 as well. Our chronicler provides further details later on. Of great interest is the report by our author of the sultan's initiative in settling in Hungary former Marranos who had found refuge in Turkey, where they openly returned to Judaism. Immediately following the Turkish conquest Jews were forced to emigrate from Hungary to the Balkans and Turkey in compliance with the Turkish policy of *sürgün*. [The policy of *sürgün* forced Jews to emigrate and resettle in another part of the Ottoman Empire. —TRANS.] See G. Kaldy-Nagy, "Contribution to the Jews of Buda in 1526: Banishment or Resettlement?" *Occident and Orient, A Tribute to the Memory of A. Scheiber* (Budapest and Leiden, 1988), 257–60; J. R. Hacker, "The Ottoman System of Sürgün and Its Influence on the Jewish Society in the Ottoman Empire" (Hebrew), *Zion* 55 (1990): 63–65. With the stabilization of Turkish rule in Hungary, Turks, including Jews, settled in Hungary, even in its capital, Buda. See S. Rosanes, *A History of the Jews in Turkey* (Hebrew; Husiatyn, 1911), 2: 10; N. Katzburg, "On the History of the Jews in Hungary under Ottoman Rule" (Hebrew), *Sinai* 31 (1952): 339–42. Our chronicler apparently is referring to this wave of immigration.

23.  This section continues the description of the Ottoman conquest of Hungary in 1526. The author alludes here to the battle of Mohács (located on the Danube near the present-day border of Yugoslavia) on 29 August 1526. In this battle the Hungarian army met with a severe setback, and King Louis II (Ludwig), king of Hungary and Bohemia, was killed. This detail is also reported in *Zemaḥ David* 2: 388. On the battle, see Merriman, *Suleiman the Magnificent*, 86–96; as well as S. Gyorgy, *A Török hóditók elleni védelem üsye a doźsa Parasztháborutól Mohacsig* (Budapest, 1952). The chronicler's report of "80,000" Hungarian casualties is greatly inflated; they

woiwode    *vajda* in Hungarian, meaning ruler. See *Chronicle*, nos. 28, 37.
[ . . . ]   The meaning of the Hebrew word *(gdvfyɔ)* is unclear.
**Pressburg**   present-day Bratislava.
**Theben**   Deveny.
**Tyrnau**   present-day Trnava.

**Romagna**   a region in central Italy.

[24] 5287 [1527] – All the Hungarians elected a king, known as the *woiwode*, [ . . . ], the son of Stephan [Zapolya], who took possession of all the Hungarian cities. The Bohemians and the [inhabitants of the] cities of Austria, Moravia, and Silesia jointly elected a king named Ferdinand, the brother of Emperor Charles, may he be exalted. In all these cities there was fear of the threat of war. May God nullify their [evil] intentions! Later that year Ferdinand took the field, capturing several cities, specifically Pressburg, Theben, and Tyrnau.

[25] 5287 [1527] – Emperor Charles V, may he be exalted, campaigned in Italy, capturing greater Rome, arresting the pope and many called cardinals, imprisoning them in his land, called Spain. He killed several hundred people in the district of Romagna, and destroyed the city of Rome, leaving it desolate, without inhabitants [Jer. 2:15; 9:10]. Not even a quarter of the population remained, for they were all killed.

numbered no more than 28,000. See A. Lhotsky, *Das Zeitalter des Hauses Österreich* (Vienna, 1971), 179–85.

24. Following the decisive Ottoman victory in Hungary, central Europe was partitioned into two kingdoms. Hungary was under Ottoman rule, with Sultan Suleiman appointing Johann (Janos) Zapolya, the son of "Stephan" Zapolya—an important commander in the Hungarian army, as *woiwode* (in Hungarian *vajda*, ruler). The chronicler subsequently refers to the king of Hungary as "the ruler, the *woiwode*" (see *Chronicle*, nos. 28, 37, 38). The other kingdom of central Europe, comprised of Bohemia, Austria, Moravia, and Silesia, was ruled by Ferdinand of the house of Habsburg, archduke of Austria, the brother of Emperor Charles V, and the brother-in-law of the previous Hungarian monarch, Louis II. (On this monarch, see below.) See Lhotsky, *Das Zeitalter*, 202ff. In that year Ferdinand succeeded in capturing a thin strip of western Hungary, including, as mentioned here, the cities of Pressburg, Theben, and Tyrnau.

25. This refers to the *"Sacco di Roma,"* or Sack of Rome, of May 1527. In the course of the fierce military engagement in Italy between the Spanish king, Charles V, and the

[26] 5287 [1527] – On Tuesday, the 15th of Tammuz [14 June], there was a severe snowstorm.

[27] 5288 [1528] – Almost no snow fell during the snowy season; during the entire winter it snowed lightly only once or twice, lasting only an hour. There was pestilence in the world. Heaven spare us!

## [Fol. 5v]

[28] 5288 [1528] – King Ferdinand, may he be exalted, journeyed to the cities of Hungary [ . . . ], negotiating with [ . . . ] the governors of each city, who recognized his sovereignty. He waged war on Hungary for several days, and deposed the ruler, the *woiwode* [*vajda*], wresting all [Hungary] from his hands.

[29] 5288 [1528] – The Jewish residents of Rhodes ruled the city, as if it were theirs. On the High Holidays, when [the Jews] prayed, the Christians withdrew from the city, erecting [temporary] edifices outside the city [ . . . ] and the Jews dwelt in the city.

**High Holidays** literally "the Days of Awe," referring to the holidays of Rosh Hashanah (the New Year) and Yom Kippur (the Day of Atonement). —TRANS. [ . . . ] The meaning of the Hebrew phrase is unclear.

French monarch, François I, Charles's army invaded Rome, destroying the city and imprisoning Pope Clement VII in the Castel Sant'Angelo, and not in Spain, as reported in our chronicle. See L. Pastor, *History of the Popes* (London, 1910) 9: 306–423; J. Hook, *The Sack of Rome, 1527* (London, 1972). See also the various monographs on Charles V; for example, G. von Schwarzenfeld, *Charles V, Father of Europe* (London, 1957), 141–45. See also *Chronicle*, no. 31.

26–27. ———

28. The author alludes to the struggle for the Hungarian crown between Zapolya, king of Hungary, and Ferdinand I. Ferdinand captured Buda on 3 November 1527 (the beginning of the Jewish year 5288), and was crowned as king of those sections of Hungary that he had captured. See F. B. Buchholtz, *Geschichte der Regierung Ferdinand der ersten* (Vienna, 1832), 3: 187–212. For a summary of Ferdinand's career, see Bosl, *Handbuch* 2: 143–63.

29. In 1522, the Turks captured the island of Rhodes from the Knights of Rhodes (the Order of the Hospital of St. John of Jerusalem). See E. Brockman, *The Two Sieges of*

**another faith** Anabaptism.
The second part of this section (the last two lines of fol. 5v and twelve lines on fol. 6r) contains many erasures, making it indecipherable.

[30] 5288 [1528] – In Ashkenaz [Germany] another faith spread, which prescribed a second baptism, regarding the first as worthless, for an infant has no understanding of the reason for baptism. They gathered great numbers [of people] and rebaptized them. Conversely, they did righteous acts, may God forgive me [for saying so]. They fulfilled the command-

---

*Rhodes, 1480–1522* (London, 1969), 111ff.; Merriman, *Suleiman the Magnificent*, 50–75. Following the Turkish conquest, the Jewish population of the island increased significantly because of the sultan's direct encouragement. See Joseph ha-Kohen, *Emeq ha-Bakha*, 70 (May, *Vale of Tears*, 75). Many Jews, including Spanish refugees, arrived from Salonika, and played an important role in the economic life of the city. See S. Marcus, "The History of the Jews of Rhodes under the Knights Hospitalers of St. John" (Hebrew), *Oṣar Yehudey Sefarad* 2 (1959): 66–68; M. Benayahu, *Relation[s] Between Greek and Italian Jewry* (Hebrew; Tel Aviv, 1980), 334–36; Hacker, "The Ottoman System of Sürgün," 59–63. In this context, R. David Gans writes: "[5]283 [1522/3]. The Turkish sultan, Suleiman, took the island of Rhodes, which had been a strong fortress for the Christians, by force. Afterwards, many Jews migrated there, living in safety to this day" (*Zemaḥ David* 2: 386). This emphasis on the large numbers and high status of the Jews on the island, following the defeat of the Knights of St. John who had persecuted them, may be an expression of the innermost hopes of Bohemian Jewry. Such a description of the capture of Rhodes may reflect an era of peace between the emperor and the sultan, who signed a treaty concerning Rhodes in 1606. See *Chronicle*, no. 74.

30.    The Hebrew word *shmad* used here refers to baptism. The entry concerns the Anabaptist ("rebaptizer") movement, founded in Germany in the 1520s. One of the principal doctrines of the sect is that only conscious believers may be baptized. Infant baptism therefore is worthless and rebaptism must be performed in adulthood. See G. H. Williams, *The Radical Reformation* (Philadelphia, 1961); E. G. Léonard, *A History of Protestantism* (London, 1965) 1: 97–99, and its detailed bibliography, 388–93. Our author alludes to the intense attraction of this sect to Judaism: "They desired to learn the laws of Moses . . . not accepting all the dogmas of Catholicism." Judaism noticeably influenced the doctrines of this movement. See L. I. Newman, *Jewish Influence on Christian Reform Movements* (New York, 1925), 470–71, 618; Baron, *Social and Religious History* 13: 242–47. The chronicler stresses the king's persecution of this sect: "The king, may he be exalted, was informed [of this heresy] by the archbishops, and decreed that each city arrest the [Anabaptists]." Indeed, the Austrian, Moravian, and Bohemian Anabaptists were persecuted severely by Ferdinand I, who even had some members of this sect executed in Vienna and Brünn (Moravia) in 1528. See Williams, *The Radical Reformation*, 149–80, 218–33, esp. 227–29, 231; Bosl, *Handbuch* 2: 120. More about the persecution of the Anabaptists appears below, notes to *Chronicle* nos. 47–48.

ment "Let him live by your side as your
kinsman" [Lev. 25:36], providing each
other's basic needs. They desired to learn
the laws of Moses, but maintained their
[belief] in Jesus, although not accepting all
the dogmas of Catholicism. The king, may
he be exalted, was informed [of this heresy]
by the archbishops, and decreed that each
city arrest the [Anabaptists]. He wished to
execute them for their beliefs. In several
places, members of this sect were caught
and bound in unspeakably heavy bonds,
but they disregarded [their shackles, say-
ing] the soul belongs to the Almighty and
the body is a thing of naught. There were
disturbances among the peasants in the
land and all agreed [ . . . ]

## [Fol. 6r]

[31]  5288 [1528] – The French king took the
pope from Spain and elevated him to his
former position. They did battle against
the emperor, may he be exalted, in Italy;
the French king and the pope joined
forces against the emperor, divesting him
of much [territory]. The emperor subse-

---

31.  The chronicler reiterates the military engagement between France and Spain in Italy
and the Sack of Rome in 1527, which he mistakenly assigns here to 1528 (see
*Chronicle*, no. 25). Pope Clement VII was imprisoned in the Castel Sant'Angelo on the
Tiber, and not in Spain as repeated here (see n. 25 above). Moreover, it was not
the "French king" who restored the pope; it was Charles V (see *Chronicle*, no. 32). The
chronicler adds information on the suffering of Roman Jewry during the course of
these events, reporting the ". . . killing [of] several people, [both] Jews and Romans."
Minimal information on this attack on Roman Jewry is found in other sources as well.
R. Joseph ha-Kohen states laconically: "Rome's splendor was totally lost. Also the Jews
were handed over to plunder and several of them lost their lives." See *Emeq ha-Bakha*,
70 (May, *Vale of Tears*, 76); *Divrey ha-Yamim*, fols. 178v–179r (Bialloblotzky, *Chronicles of Rabbi Joseph* 2: 72–73, par. 686). R. Elijah Lévita (Baḥur) alludes to these

quently captured Rome, killing several people, [both] Jews and Romans, in the city of Rome, placing the pope under arrest away from [Rome] until the present.

[32]  5289 [1529] – The emperor, may he be exalted, restored the pope to his seat in Rome, with the [pope's] recognition of [the emperor's] dominion.

[33]  5289 [1529] – On Rosh Ḥodesh Sivan [9 May] there was a blood libel in the city of Pösing. All the [Jewish] men, women, and children were arrested and tortured with unheard-of severity because of our iniquities; men and women, and even a pregnant woman whose abdomen ruptured,

---

events in the introduction to his book *Masoret ha-Masoret* (Venice, 1538), 10; see G. E. Weil, *Elie Lévita* (Leiden, 1963), 106–9. A more detailed report is found in a 1539 responsum of R. Isaac b. Emanuel (de) Lattes of Carpentras concerning a dispute between the "holy community of Aragon" and the "holy community of Castile" in Rome. He writes: "When God allowed Rome to be plundered, and Israel was looted as well, the [Jewish] communities were greatly reduced in number, and many died. Some died a natural death, others [died] by the sword, or by starvation. Many wandered afar due to the perils of the war. Not even a minyan remained in the synagogues for prayer and marriage; moreover, many synagogues were destroyed. [The Jews] were forced to mingle, family with family, [with Jews from] Aragon uniting with Catalonians and French Castilians." See S. Schwarzfuchs, "Maaseh be-Kehillat Roma be-Maḥaṣitah ha-Rishonah shel ha-Meah ha-16," in *Scritti in Memoria di Enzo Sereni* (Jerusalem, 1970), 137. Concerning attacks on Italian Jews in locations outside of Rome during that year, see A. David, "New Documents Concerning the History of Italian Jewry under the Shadow of Sixteenth-Century Catholic Reaction" (Hebrew), *Tarbiz* 49 (1980): 366–68.

32.  Pope Clement VII, deposed when Spanish forces invaded Rome in 1527, remained imprisoned for seven months and was subsequently exiled to various locations in Italy. At a later date, 14 October 1528, the pope and Charles V were reconciled. The pope was restored to his seat in Rome in February 1530 following a joint meeting in Bologna, where he agreed to recognize fully Charles V's hegemony over the Holy Roman Empire. See Pastor, *History of the Popes* 10: 1–99, and the various monographs on Charles V, for example, von Schwarzenfeld, *Charles V,* 148–49.

33.  In Pösing (Boesing, Bezinok), a small town, some thirty Jews were executed on the 13th of Sivan 5289 (21 May 1529) as a result of a typical blood libel accusation. This affair is noted in other sources, both Jewish and general. R. Joseph of Rosheim briefly describes the event in his short diary (Kracauer, "Rabbi Joselmann de Rosheim," 90),

causing her to miscarry. The Jews confessed, implicating Jews of other cities [as
well] and there was unspeakably great danger in all the cities. On the eve of Shavuot

[Fol. 6v]

there were [ . . . ] executions by burning
and the smoke of thirty-three [Jewish]
souls reached the heavens. And the Jews in
other places were in great danger. [ . . . ]
The Jews banded together, taking their
moneybags to bribe the king and many
lords with a large sum, several thousands,
in an attempt, with God's help, to nullify

---

where he relates his role in preventing the spread of the disturbances. Two lists of the
martyrs are known from two manuscripts: the now-lost old *pinkas* of the Kraków
burial society, published in Sokolow, *Ha-Asif* 6 (1894): 133, and in D. Kaufmann,
"Die Märtyrer des pösinger Autodafés von 1529," *MGWJ* 38 (1894): 426–29; and a
variant list found in Prague Jewish Museum MS. 64, published in Sheiber, "The
Martyrs of Phising," 227–30.

Non-Jewish sources shed much light on the details and background of this blood
libel. In 1540, the evangelist Andreas Osiander strongly denounced blood libels, and
his remarks reflect the impact of the events at Pösing. He also provides additional
details concerning the blood libel and its aftermath. See M. Stern, *Andreas Osianders
Schrift über die Blutbeschuldigungen* (Berlin, 1903), vii, xv, xvii, 32ff. For other
documents relating to this blood libel, see M. H. Friedländer, *Zur Geschichte der
Blutbeschuldigungen gegen die Juden im Mittelalter und der Neuzeit (1171–1882)*
(Frankfurt am Main, 1883), 15–16; H. L. Strack, *Der Blutaberglaube in der Menschheit* (Munich, 1892), 120–21; S. Stern, *Josel von Rosheim* (Stuttgart, 1959), 72–75.

The chronicler dates the arrests stemming from the blood libel to Rosh Ḥodesh
Sivan 5289 (9 May 1529), and notes that the Jews were "tortured with unheard-of
severity. . . . [and] confessed, implicating Jews of other cities [as well]." From the
non-Jewish sources it appears that initially a wealthy Jew named Esslein Ausch was
arrested. Under torture he reportedly confessed to the murder of the child, at the same
time implicating others, including Jews from the city of Marchegg, Austria
(Niederöstereich), as alluded to by our chronicler. According to R. Joseph of Rosheim:
"All those Jews in Moravia were arrested." Thus, this accusation was not confined
solely to Pösing. It extended as far as Moravia, as implied by our chronicle: "There
was unspeakably great danger in all the cities." The chronicler establishes the eve of
Shavuot, or the 5th of Sivan, as the date of the burning, whereas all other sources,
Jewish and non-Jewish, cite the 13th of Sivan. The chronicle reports that thirty-three

**Kasnalna Kasanzna[?]** We have no knowledge of this person, nor even the exact spelling of his name.
**Laudowitz[?]** an unidentified town.

their evil intentions [regarding] the remaining prisoners who were not guilty. Nonetheless, due to our iniquities several children still remain among them to this day, who cannot be saved even now. Rumors were heard in the land, which I will not record, not knowing whether they be true or false. And it was said that the commander of the king's army named Kasnalna Kasanzna[?] took the field against Hungary with a large force; at the same time all the royal governors held a council in the town of Laudowitz[?]. Concurrently, one of the king's commanders died at Tyrnau, and was replaced by a new head, an adversary and enemy [Esther 7:6 —Trans.] [of the Jews] who tried to persecute the Jews, Heaven forbid, based on the confessions of the burned martyrs of Pösing. May God avenge them! But the Holy One, Blessed be He, nullified his [evil] intent.

---

Jewish souls were burned, general sources thirty, and R. Joseph of Rosheim "thirty-six souls." The *pinkas* of the Kraków burial society enumerates twenty-four martyrs, while the manuscript in the Prague Jewish Museum enumerates thirty-one. Our chronicler's allusion to the forced baptism of Jewish children as a result of this blood libel accusation is supported by non-Jewish sources as well. The chronicler also notes that the Jews attempted to intercede with the authorities in order to secure the release of the prisoners. "The Jews banded together, taking their moneybags to bribe the king and many lords with a large sum . . . in an attempt, with God's help, to nullify their evil intentions [regarding] the remaining prisoners who were not guilty." This comment certainly refers to R. Joseph of Rosheim's intensive intercession on behalf of the prisoners. He writes: "I had to bring copies of old writs of privilege from popes and emperors to the city of Günzberg, where I copied them, with the addition of words of apology, into a booklet, and I forwarded them to the king and his servants, and the justice of our cause became known, and they released the prisoners." The Prague chronicler continues his account by relating that a further attempt to harm the Jews was made, "based on the confessions of the burned martyrs of Pösing . . . . But the Holy One, Blessed be He, nullified his [evil] intent."

[34] 5289 [1529] — In all the lands there was a new accusation against the Jews, one not found in the Pentateuch, impugning that they spy on the emperor, may he be exalted, for the Ottoman sultan. In consequence, there was a plot to deny the Jews their rights, leaving them unprotected and liable to massacre and extermination, Heaven forbid! All the governors of the lands intended to issue an edict of expulsion, Heaven forbid, with the king's approval, may he be exalted. But God, Blessed be He, nullified their evil intent.

**Pentateuch** This refers to the admonitory chapters in Lev. 26:14–43 and Deut. 28:15–68.

34. Reports of rumors that the Jews aided the Ottoman conquest of Hungary and parts of the Habsburg dominions (see *Chronicle,* nos. 22–23 for an account of the campaign) are well documented in general sources. See Baron, *Social and Religious History* 13: 258–59; 444–45. At a somewhat later date, Luther accused the Jews of expressing their hatred of Christianity by supporting the Turks. See Lewin, *Luthers Stellung zu den Juden,* 74–75.

Our chronicler relates that because of these rumors Jews were subject to expulsion and extermination. The expulsion decree, however, was rescinded. In the words of the chronicle, "But God, Blessed be He, nullified their evil intent." In his diary, R. Joseph of Rosheim recounts the measures taken to nullify the decree: "In [5]290 [1530] there was an outcry among the nations [saying] the Jews spy for the Turks. These accusations reached the ears of our masters the emperor and the king, may they be exalted, and they disenfranchised us, forbidding us entry into several countries. With the backing of the [Jewish] communities, I prepared and arranged a booklet [containing] our words of apology. With the help of God [I presented it] before the two monarchs in the city of Innsbruck. And Joseph found favor [in their eyes], and they willingly accepted our words of apology, validating our writs of privilege" (see Kracauer, "R. Joselmann de Rosheim," 90). Apparently, R. Joseph of Rosheim's active intervention to prevent the expulsion of the Jews had far-reaching influence. When accusations of spying for the Turks were voiced against the Jews at the Augsburg Reichstag in 1530, both Charles V and his brother Ferdinand I forcefully rejected the charges. See Steinherz, "Expulsion of the Jews," 85 n. 45, 91. Similar accusations subsequently were raised in the course of anti-Jewish agitation in Bohemia, which led to the expulsion of the Jews in 1541 (see *Chronicle,* no. 51). Spying for the Turks was one of the charges enumerated by King Ferdinand in the instructions sent on 12 September to his agents in the Landstag concerning the expulsion of the Jews. See Steinherz, "Expulsion of the Jews," 85 n. 45, 91; Baron, *Social and Religious History* 13: 261.

Similar accusations of Jewish treachery during Moslem-Christian wars are well known. They surfaced during the Moslem conquest of Erez Israel from the Byzantines (634–638 c.e.). See M. Avi-Yonah, *The Jews under Roman and Byzantine Rule,* 2d ed.

The author provided a
drawing of the sun illustrating the degree of the
eclipse.

[35]  5289 [1528] – On the 29th day of Kislev
[11 December], a rainbow was visible in
the sky.

[36]  5290 [1530] – On Tuesday, Rosh Ḥodesh
Nisan [29 March] in the sixth hour of the
watch [at noon], there was a black eclipse
of the sun, [with the sun] almost totally
covered like this, lasting for nearly two
hours.

## [Fol 7r]

[37]  5290 [1529] – The aforementioned ruler,
the *woiwode*, mustered a strong force numbering several thousands, and attacked the
cities of Hungary with the support of the
Ottoman sultan's innumerable forces, capturing several cities and burning a number

---

(Jerusalem, 1984), 273–74. The accusation that the Jews betrayed Visigothic Spain to
the Arabs in 711 was formulated only after the Reconquest. See E. Ashtor, *The Jews of
Moslem Spain* (Philadelphia, 1973) 1: 18, 407 n. 5.

35–36.  ———

37.  King Ferdinand, who sought to gain hegemony over Hungary, succeeded in taking
Buda on 3 November 1527, and was crowned king in the sectors under his control
(see *Chronicle*, no. 28). In this struggle for dominion of Hungary, the Hungarian king,
Zapolya, was backed by the Ottoman sultan, Suleiman the Magnificent. As related in
our chronicle, the sultan and his forces, with the aid of the Hungarian ruler, "the
woiwode" (Zapolya), attempted to conquer the Habsburg kingdom and its capital,
Vienna. Gaining control of the Donau River, they reached the gates of Vienna on 27
September 1529 (the beginning of the Jewish year 5290). The Ottoman Turks laid siege
to Vienna for more than two weeks, until 14 October (Marḥeshvan, as reported in the
chronicle), when they retreated, largely because of bad weather conditions. On this
military campaign, see Merriman, *Suleiman The Magnificent,* 97–125; C. Turetschek,
"Die Türkenpolitik Ferdinands I von 1529 bis 1532" (Ph.D. diss., Vienna, 1968). Both
David Gans, *Ẓemaḥ David,* 389–90, and Joseph ha-Kohen, *Divrey ha-Yamim,* fols.
190v–192r (Bialloblotzky, *Chronicles of Rabbi Joseph* 2: 105–9, par. 747–55), mention the battle at the gates of Vienna, with the latter providing a more detailed
description. The chronicler's dates are accurate, as is the description of the general
situation; however, the data concerning the size of the participating forces apparently
are based on inaccurate estimates. Cf. the numerical data in Joseph ha-Kohen's *Divrey
ha-Yamim.*

of villages. King Ferdinand, may he be exalted, ordered the conscription of one of every five men in all the cities [of his dominion], assembling [a force] of several thousands. In the interim, the Turkish forces marched on Pressburg and Vienna, gaining control of the Donau River, marching on Vienna twice with several thousand soldiers. The forces [of the Turks and Ferdinand] engaged [in battle]. On a single day thirty thousand Turkish soldiers fell in battle, and from King [Ferdinand's] forces, may he be exalted, fifteen hundred [fell]. The other cities of Bohemia, Moravia, Silesia, and Austria, assembled their forces, and several armies were encamped near Vienna. The Turks attacked the people of Vienna several times, without capturing any territory. Consequently, the Turks retreated in the month of Marḥeshvan 5290 [October 1529].

[38] 5290 [1530] – On Rosh Ḥodesh Adar [29 January], King [Ferdinand's]—may he be exalted—commander-in-chief marched on the city of Gran in Hungary with a force of five thousand soldiers. Upon receiving word of the force of five thousand, the [Hungarian] ruler, the so-called *woiwode*, attacked the invading army, pursuing it and slaughtering three thousand of its men. The remnant fled to Pressburg.

**Gran**  Esztergom in Hungarian.

38. The chronicle relates the continued struggle between Ferdinand and Zapolya for control of Hungary. A few months following the repulsion of the Turkish forces besieging Vienna, Ferdinand, king of Bohemia, made a second attempt to reach Buda. He concentrated his forces in Gran, north of Buda. His army was routed severely by Zapolya's forces, with the remnant taking refuge in Pressburg, in closer proximity to Vienna. See Buchholtz, *Geschichte der Regierung* 4: 65ff; and Turetschek, "Die Türkenpolitik," 130ff.

[39] 5290 [1530] – The pope crowned the King [Charles V as Holy Roman Emperor], may he be exalted, in the great city of Rome. [In order to become the German monarch] the emperor swore vengeance on [his enemy] the king of France.

[40] 5291 [1530] – On the 9th of Tevet [29 December], a rainbow was visible in the sky.

## [Fol. 7v]

[41] 5291 [1530] – It [rained] for nearly eighty days, from Marḥeshvan [October/November] for weeks [ . . . ]; it was hardly cold at all, and everything was expensive, even [ . . . ].

**Skhum**   Rome; see historical notes.

[42] 5291 [1530] – [Reports] of a great torrent were heard, in which several thousand people drowned, and hundreds of houses in the great city of Skhum were [washed away].

39.  This refers to the coronation of Charles V as Holy Roman Emperor by Pope Clement VII in Bologna (and not in Rome as stated here) on 22 February 1530. Cf. von Schwarzenfeld, *Charles V,* 148–51. The coronation is also described by Joseph ha-Kohen, *Divrey ha-Yamim,* fol. 193v (Bialloblotzky, *Chronicles of Rabbi Joseph* 2: 112–13, par. 765). The concluding sentence apparently means that the emperor, in order to secure his position in the Holy Roman Empire (here termed "Germany"), swore to exact vengeance on his principal enemy, François I of France (king 1515–1547), whom he had engaged in fierce battle in Italy several years earlier.

40–41. ──────

42.  This refers to a flood in Rome, called "Skhum" by the chronicler for no immediately obvious reason. This natural disaster is described by Joseph ha-Kohen, *Divrey ha-Yamim,* fols. 200v–201r (which is the basis for the account in *Ẓemaḥ David* 2: 390). Joseph ha-Kohen states: "And in the eighth month, on the sixth of the month, the Lord caused it to rain upon Rome and its environs, the portion of their cup. And the windows of heaven were opened. And on the seventh day the fountains of the deep were broken up, and the waters of the flood were upon the earth. And the waters prevailed, and they increased much upon the earth; and the river Tiber came into the city. . . . And the Tiber increased more and more, and overflowed in abundance, and houses filled with every thing good it cast to the ground. And the houses of the city were filled with mire and dirt. . . . And there died from the overflowing of the proud

[43] The Emperor, may he be exalted, laid seige to the city of Ofen [Budapest] with nearly five thousand men, capturing and possessing it.

[44] 5292 [1532] – In the month of Elul [August] there was great agitation because the Turks came with a great, innumerable multitude, so great it could not be measured, and there was trepidation in the cities. Consequently, Emperor Charles [V], may he be exalted, and his brother King Ferdinand, may he be exalted, ordered all the lands [in their dominions] to conscript one of every ten men. And they assembled a multitude, approximately three hundred times one thousand from all the cities of their kingdom. Not one lord of a village was missing, but each came with his men; and the multitude was so great that it erased the memory of former armies. It was incomparable. At this time nearly ten thousand

waters, about three thousand souls of men" (Bialloblotzky, *Chronicles of Rabbi Joseph* 2: 133–35, par. 801). Both sources emphasize the large number of people that perished, with the Prague chronicle reporting "several thousand," and Joseph ha-Kohen, "three thousand." The use of the word "Skhum" for Rome in the chronicle is puzzling. Perhaps it refers to the sack of Rome by the armies of Charles V in 1527 (see *Chronicle*, nos. 25, 31), known in Italian as the *"Sacco di Roma."* However this proposed explanation is tentative and requires further investigation.

43. In 1530, King Ferdinand I succeeded in capturing Ofen (Buda). Cf. Buchholtz, *Geschichte der Regierung* 4: 69ff.

44. Sultan Suleiman began his several-months-long journey to Vienna on 26 April 1532, arriving there on 28 August 1532 (in Elul, as stated here). However, following his defeat in several fierce military engagements, Suleiman retreated with the remnants of his army. The military campaign affected nearby cities as well. As mentioned in the chronicle, a fierce battle raged in Linz, a city located west of Vienna. On the course of the battle, see Buchholtz, *Geschichte der Regierung* 4: 93ff; Merriman, *Suleiman the Magnificent*, 112ff; von Schwarzenfeld, *Charles V,* 159–64; Turetschek, "Die Türkenpolitik." Suleiman's trip and campaign against Vienna are described at length in Joseph ha-Kohen, *Divrey ha-Yamim*, fols. 202v–206r (Bialloblotzky, *Chronicles of Rabbi Joseph* 2: 139–48, par. 807–32), and briefly by David Gans, *Zemah David* 2: 391.

**Linz**   a city west of
Vienna.

Turks surrounded Vienna, causing great
losses. The people of Vienna attacked [the
Turks], killing all; not one survived. And it
was reported that several thousand Turks
were only two miles from the city of Linz,
but the people of Linz attacked from one
direction, and the [people] of Vienna from
the other, killing them all, with the battle
waxing fiercer daily.

## [Fol. 8r]

The handwritten Hebrew
in fol. 8r is difficult to read
and ellipses are given
where the text was impos-
sible to reconstruct.
—TRANS.

[45]  5293 [1532] – On the eighth day of the
month of Marḥeshvan [8 October 1532],
[ . . . ] the enemies of the Turks took
nearly three thousand ships [ . . . ] Men
from the city of Pressburg killed [ . . . ]
people of many towns. At this time Emperor Charles came with his brother the
king, may he be exalted, to the city of
Vienna with a great multitude, [number-
ing] approximately three times one hundred and forty-three thousand, and there
was great fear. They were there nearly ten
days [ . . . ] and the emperor sent his men
home without a battle [ . . . ] There was
great [bewilderment] everywhere [as to]
why he mustered them and then sent them
home. And the emperor, may he be exalted, sent nearly eighty thousand Spanish
mercenaries against the cities of Hungary,

---

45.   In an attempt to restore order to the kingdom and to renew their campaign to acquire
dominion over Hungary, Emperor Charles V and his brother Ferdinand entered
Vienna. See Merriman, *Suleiman the Magnificent,* 119–20; Turetschek, "Die Türkenpolitik."

commanding them to kill and to plunder all their money; in return they would be freed, and entitled to keep their booty.

[46] 5293 [1532] – In Marḥeshvan [October] a star appeared in the eastern part of the sky during the [first] watch; it had a long tail and was ascendant. The people called it a morning star.

**morning star** Here the author provided an illustration.

[47] 5295 [1535] – The king, may he be exalted, commanded that all the rebaptizers [Anabaptists] be expelled, but they paid him no heed. They increased greatly from day to day, becoming innumerable. Among them there were extremely wealthy men dwelling in cities and unwalled towns throughout Moravia, and they became very powerful.

[48] 5296 [1536] – The king, may he be exalted, commanded his officials and courtiers to proclaim this faith as proscribed everywhere in his kingdom,

## [Fol. 8v]

in all the farflung parts of his land. They [the Anabaptists] were seized by fear and trembling [Isa. 33:14], [for although] they had spread throughout [the land], they had to leave their houses, vineyards, fields, and animals and go despairingly from the land of their sojourn, not knowing which way to turn, becoming separated from their brethren, scattered here and there.

46. ———

47–48. King Ferdinand I continued to persecute the Anabaptists, who had a major center in Moravia (see *Chronicle*, no. 30). The chief leader of this sect was Jakob Hutter, who attracted a large following in Moravia. Hutter was executed on 19 November 1535. See Williams, *The Radical Reformation,* 417–34.

Nos. 49–50 are accompanied by drawings of the solar and lunar eclipses, and the solar corona as they appeared to the author.

[49] 5296 [1536] – On the eve of Rosh Ḥodesh Tammuz [18 June], on Sunday, there was a solar eclipse in the second hour, that is, two hours after midday. [The sun] remained covered for nearly an hour and a half, appearing thus. That same night there was a lunar eclipse from nightfall, and the moon was covered for nearly two hours, appearing thus.

[50] 5297 [1537] – On Thursday, the 14th of Sivan [24 May], at midday, there was a solar eclipse lasting for nearly two hours, with a halo around the sun, appearing thus.

## [Fol. 9r]

[51] 5301 [1541] – King Ferdinand, may he be exalted, expelled [the Jews] from all the cities of Bohemia, and here in Prague only

49. The author erred. The eve of Rosh Ḥodesh Tammuz 5296 fell on Monday and not on Sunday. This type of error is not uncommon.

50. ———

51. The expulsion decree was issued by Ferdinand I on 12 September 1541 (the 20th of Elul 5301) as a result of pressure by the local populace. The deadline for departure was 23 April 1542 (5302). See Bondy and Dworsky, *Zur Geschichte der Juden* 1: 336. Regarding the expulsion and its causes, see Steinherz, "Expulsion of the Jews," 70–92; Baron, *Social and Religious History* 13: 260–66, 444–48.

Information on the expulsion of the Jews from Bohemia is available from other Jewish sources as well: (1) Joseph ha-Kohen, *Divrey ha-Yamim*, fol. 268r–v (Bialloblotzky, *Chronicles of Rabbi Joseph* 2: 337–38, par. 1051–54), and in a revised, briefer version in *Emeq ha-Bakha*, 75–76 (May, *Vale of Tears*, 81). See my comments in the introduction. (2) Gedaliah ibn Yaḥya, *Shalshelet ha-Kabbalah*, fol. 117r, and in an expanded version in Moscow, Ginzburg collection MS. 652, fol. 213r–v. His account is based on that of Joseph ha-Kohen. (3) Samuel Usque, *A Consolation for the Tribulations of Israel*, trans. G. I. Gelbart (New York, 1964), third dialogue, 404–6. Usque mistakenly ascribes the decree to 1306. See the translator's comments, 407 nn. 1–2. See also *Shalshelet ha-Kabbalah*, Moscow MS. 652, fol. 214r. (4) David Gans, *Ẓemaḥ David* 1: 139 (see my comments in the introduction). (5) R. Abraham b. Avigdor, "An Elegy on the Expulsion" (Hebrew), published in German translation by L. Zunz in *Synagogale Poesie des Mittelalters* (Berlin, 1855), 57. The

ten [Jewish] householders remained. Subsequently, he allowed them to return, with
the help of God.

---

original has been published several times. See I. Davidson, Oṣar ha-Shirah ve-ha-
Piyyut (New York, 1924), 1: 279, no. 6111. (6) Jacob b. Eliezer Ulma, "An Elegy on
the Expulsion" (Hebrew), in Y. L. Bialer, Min Hagenazim: Description of Manuscripts
and Historical Documents (Jerusalem, 1967) 1: 63–69. (7) Joseph of Rosheim. In his
diary (Kracauer, Rabbi Joselmann de Rosheim, 93), R. Joseph relates how he tried, to
no avail, to effect the cancellation of the decree. See my comments in the introduction.

Our chronicler notes that "here, in Prague, only ten [Jewish] householders remained." This information, found in Ẓemaḥ David as well, receives additional confirmation from general documentation, which indicates that the king allowed fifteen
Jews to remain in Prague for an additional year in order to manage the Jewish property
in the Judenstraße. See Steinherz, "Expulsion of the Jews," 87–88. Joseph ha-Kohen
and David Gans attribute the expulsion order to allegations that acts of arson were
committed by Jews in various parts of Bohemia (to be discussed below). Both our
chronicle and the two previously mentioned sources state that after a time the king
permitted the expellees to return. In this regard, David Gans adds: "But after a short
time, within less than a year, the king and the people discovered on whose account
this misfortune had come upon them, and realizing that the Jews had been accused
falsely, spoke favorably of them . . . and [the Jews] returned to their country and
birthplace as before" (Ẓemaḥ David 1: 139).

Characteristically, the chronicler makes no allusion to the underlying causes moti-
vating the king to issue the expulsion decree. Joseph ha-Kohen and David Gans
attribute the decree to false accusations against the Jews concerning acts of arson in
many locations: "in many towns, large and small, in Ashkenaz," according to Joseph
ha-Kohen, and "in all the cities of Bohemia," according to David Gans. The general
documentation supports the view that the major factor was the charge of arson. See
Steinherz, "Expulsion of the Jews," 83, 89–92. Samuel Usque ascribes the expulsion
to a blood libel accusation, but this explanation has no support in general or Jewish
sources, making its accuracy doubtful. Other contributing factors were intense pressure by the subjects in various counties in Bohemia to remove the Jewish presence,
and the oft-repeated accusation of Jewish aid to the Ottoman Turks in their military
engagement with Ferdinand (see Chronicle, no. 34).

Baron suggests that Ferdinand also may have been motivated by anti-Semitic feelings imbibed in his father's house, the Spanish royal court (see Baron, Social and
Religious History 13: 446 no. 63). Recently it has been suggested that Ferdinand's true
motive for the expulsion was his fear that a continued Jewish presence in Bohemia
would enhance the already strong influence of the Jews on radical protestant sects like
the Anabaptists and Sabbatarians, who had a large following in Moravia and Bohemia
(see Chronicle, nos. 30, 47).

It appears that in addition to local pressure to expel the Jews, it was Jewish influence
on Protestant sects that tipped the scales, leading Ferdinand to solve the Jewish
problem by expulsion. See J. Herman, "The Conflict between Jewish and Non-Jewish
Population in Bohemia before the 1541 Banishment," Judaica Bohemiae 6 (1970):

[52]  5319 [1559] – Due to our iniquities, there
was another decree expelling [the Jews]
from all the cities of Bohemia, and here, in
Prague, only twelve [Jewish] householders
remained.

[53]  5319 [1559] – Due to our iniquities, there
was a fire in the Judenstraße here in
Prague, in which seventy-two houses were

39–45. Support for Herman's view is found in the words of Joseph ha-Kohen: "Then
Bohemia sinned against its king and its God, expelling the Jews from Bohemia and
Prague because of the wrath of the Lutherans." This juxtaposition indicates that the
author associated the emergence of Lutheranism with the expulsion.

52.   In 1557 Ferdinand I decided to expel his Jewish subjects from Bohemia. The edict was
first promulgated on 27 August 1557, but its implementation was delayed. See Bondy
and Dworsky, *Zur Geschichte der Juden* 1: 421–24, nos. 522–23. On 23 July 1558,
the king, by this time also Holy Roman Emperor (from 1558), ordered that the Jews
depart by 23 April 1559. See Bondy and Dworsky, *Zur Geschichte der Juden* 1: 430–
31, no. 590. Our chronicle refers to the latter date. Similar accounts appear in Joseph
ha-Kohen, *Divrey ha-Yamim* 3: 59; idem, *Emeq ha-Bakha*, 90 (May, *Vale of Tears*,
96–97); and David Gans, *Zemah David* 1: 141. An additional Hebrew source indicates that the decree was implemented despite a direct appeal from Pope Pius IV. See
the statement by the anonymous corrector, *Emeq ha-Bakha*, 98. Both the Prague
chronicle and David Gans specify in almost identical words that "in Prague, only
twelve [Jewish] householders remained." The royal documents indicate that Ferdinand allowed ten to twelve Jews to remain in Prague for up to a year only, in order to
collect their debts and sell their property. See Bondy and Dworsky, *Zur Geschichte der
Juden* 1: 434, no. 594. According to Joseph ha-Kohen, "some two hundred [Jewish]
householders remained, while the rest departed."
      The implementation of the edict of expulsion thus is reported in four independent
Hebrew sources. With the exception of the aforementioned decree, there are no clear
references to the expulsion of the Jews in extant royal documents relating to that year.
Further examination of the royal documents seems to indicate that Ferdinand's son
Maximilian, and his wife, succeeded in delaying the implementation of the edict until
1561. See Bondy and Dworsky, *Zur Geschichte der Juden* 1: 449–51, no. 611. The
Prague chronicle (no. 56) mentions an additional expulsion in 1561 (see note below).
Furthermore, following this chronicle entry, two events from the intervening years are
recounted, thus indicating that the Jews remained in Bohemia. Graetz, too, maintains
that the expulsion was delayed until 1561. See Graetz, *History of the Jews* 4: 584–86;
B. Brilling, "Eine Eingabe der böhmischen Judenheit vom jahre 1560," *Zeitschrift für
die Geschichte der Juden in Tschechoslowakei* 5 (1938): 59–62; Baron, *Social and
Religious History* 14: 158–59, 363.

53.   In this year the Jewish quarter was severely damaged, thus illustrating the further
deterioration in Jewish status. Both Joseph ha-Kohen and David Gans (see n. 52) note
that dozens of houses in the Judenstraße were destroyed by fire on the 17th of Tammuz
5319 (22 June 1559). Joseph ha-Kohen reports that "approximately sixty houses" were

consumed by the flames, as well as the Hochschul. This occurred on the 17th of Tammuz [22 June]. A woman named Friedel Niches perished in the fire as well, due to our iniquities.

**Hochschul** one of the Prague synagogues.

[54] 5320 [1560] – King Ferdinand, may he be exalted, was crowned emperor. He ordered the confiscation of all the [Jewish] books in Prague, and the *hazzanim* prayed from memory in the synagogue. On Monday, the 16th of Sivan [10 June] he sent [the books] to Vienna; their weight was fifty-seven talents. This was the result of accusations by apostates, and only a few books were returned.

burned, while David Gans's report agrees with the Prague chronicle, citing the loss of "seventy-two houses." The chronicle also discloses that the Hochschul was consumed by the flames as well. It was later rebuilt by the philanthropist R. Mordecai Meisel. Regarding the reconstruction of this synagogue, see *Zemah David* 1: 146, and *Chronicle*, no. 67. Our author also stresses the loss of lives resulting from the conflagration, even noting the name of a female victim. Joseph ha-Kohen adds: "And several women were also thrown into the fire" (*Divrey ha-Yamim* 3: 59; *Emeq ha-Bakha*, 90; May, *Vale of Tears*, 97).

54.  In actuality, Ferdinand I ruled the Holy Roman Empire from 1556, during the lifetime of his brother Charles V, who died 21 September 1558. Royal documents indicate that in response to pressure from anti-Jewish clerical circles, Ferdinand ordered the confiscation of Jewish books in Prague on 13 March 1560. The books were sent to Vienna for inspection by church censors. See Bondy and Dworsky, *Zur Geschichte der Juden* 1: 449–51, no. 611; Baron, *Social and Religious History* 14: 158–59, 363. The decree was implemented some three months later, on 10 June 1560, as reported in the Prague chronicle (the 16th of Sivan 5320). On 6 August 1560 the emperor ordered that the books be loaded on two wagons and returned to Prague, duty-free. See Bondy and Dworsky, *Zur Geschichte der Juden* 1: 457, no. 622. This episode is reported by Joseph ha-Kohen, *Divrey ha-Yamim* 3: 60, and David Gans, *Zemah David* 1: 141. See n. 52 above. The last two both assign these events to 5319 (1559) rather than to 1560 as in the Prague chronicle and the aforementioned official documents. The Prague chronicle ascribes the book confiscation to "accusations by apostates." Similarly, Joseph ha-Kohen reports: "An Ashkenazi apostate and scoundrel, Judah from Udena was formerly his name in Israel, went and spoke perversely of the Jews." The accounts of the Prague chronicle and David Gans differ in detail. The chronicle reports that the books weighed "fifty-seven talents"; David Gans states "eighty." In *Zemah David* we are told that "all the books were returned," whereas the Prague chronicle maintains that "only a few books were returned."

[55]  5321 [1561] – There was an expulsion from Würzburg and the surrounding settlements of that district.

[Fol. 9v]

Several words are indecipherable because the page is damaged, and the owner of the manuscript pasted a piece of paper on this section.

[56]  5321 [1561] – There was an evil royal decree [requiring] forced conversion [of the Jews] in the cities of Bohemia [ . . . ] or their departure from the kingdom of Bohemia, and taking much [ . . . ] from all the cities, and widows [ . . . ]. They withstood the temptation [to convert], leaving the cities of Bohemia between Yom Kippur and Sukkot in 5322 [September 1561]. This was at the instigation of Emperor Ferdinand.

55.  In 1561 an edict was issued expelling the Jews of Würzburg. The Jews returned to this district only in 1623. See S. Bamberger, *Geschichte der Rabbiner der Stadt und des Bezirkes Würzburg* (Wandsbek, 1905), 32ff.
56.  On 24 March 1561, Emperor Ferdinand presented Bohemian Jewry with an ultimatum—conversion or expulsion. See Bondy and Dworsky, *Zur Geschichte der Juden* 1: 457–58, no. 623. Ferdinand's decree of forced conversion was implemented only partially, for few Jews converted. See Herman, "Conflict between Jewish and non-Jewish Population," 44ff. Jews who remained faithful to their ancestral faith were forced to take up an itinerant existence. The Prague chronicle dates the departure of the exiles to September 1561 (between Yom Kippur and Sukkot). However, royal documents indicate that Jews remained in the kingdom after this date. An ordinance dated 15 December 1561 granted the Jews a final six-week extension. See Bondy and Dworsky, *Zur Geschichte der Juden* 1: 467–68, no. 635. At any rate, some of the expellees left Bohemia in 1561, as testified to by one of the leading contemporary rabbinical authorities of Prague, R. Mordecai Jaffe, the author of the *Levushim*. In the introduction to his treatise *Levush Mordecai* (Prague, 1623), a commentary on the *Shulḥan Arukh, Orah Ḥayyim* (legal code), R. Mordecai Jaffe writes: "Some time afterward, wrath came forth from the Lord [in] a decree of expulsion from my homeland, Bohemia, and the First Cause, Blessed be He, made me go into exile at the head of the expellees from the holy community of Prague in [5]321, and I went to the land of Italy." The entire episode of the return of the Jews remains obscure. Toward the end of his life (d. 1564), Ferdinand was somewhat more tolerant of the Jews remaining in Bohemia, apparently due, in large measure, to the intervention of Pope Pius IV (pope 1559–1565). See Bondy and Dworsky, *Zur Geschichte der Juden* 1: 487, no. 662; Graetz, *History of the Jews* 4: 586–87. This pope's favorable attitude toward the Jews manifested itself on several levels. See I. Sonne, *From Paul IV to Pius V* (Hebrew;

[57]  5323 [1562] — King Maximilian, may he be exalted, came here, to Prague, on Monday the 6th of Tishri [5 September], and he was crowned on *Hoshanah Rabba* [the last day of Sukkot—20 September]. In that year there was pestilence everywhere.

The Hebrew date reads on the 6th day of the new moon of Tishri.

## [Fol. 10r]

[58]  5331 [1571] — On Sunday, the 9th of Adar I [4 February], Emperor Maximilian and his wife, the empress, Madam Maria, paraded down the Judenstraße accompanied by all the royal dignitaries, [riding] on wagons called *Schlitten* in German, going from gate to gate in the twenty-second hour.

**wagons called *Schlitten*** I.e., sleds. Apparently the visit took place during the snowy season, in February.

Jerusalem, 1954), 165–75. In any case, Jewish remigration to Bohemia increased during the reign of Ferdinand's son and successor, Maximilian II, who ruled Bohemia from September 1562, and replaced his father as Holy Roman Emperor from 1564–1575. Unlike his father, Maximilian was favorably disposed toward the Jews. See Bondy and Dworsky, *Zur Geschichte der Juden* 1: 494–550, nos. 674–759; T. Jakobowitz, "Die Jüdischen Zünfte in Prag," *Jahrbuch der Gesellschaft für Geschichten der Juden in der Cechoslovakischen Republik* 8 (1936): 61–63. For a summary of this topic, see Baron, *Social and Religious History* 14: 160–62, See also S. Steinherz, "Sage und Geschichte," *Jahrbuch der Gesellschaft für Geschichte der Juden in der Cechoslovakischen Republik* 9 (1938): 138ff.

57.  Maximilian II's reign over Bohemia commenced in September 1562 (Tishri 5323) with his coronation in Prague. See V. Bibl, *Maximilian II der rätselhafte Kaiser, ein Zeitbild* (Leipzig, 1929), 101–2. For a general summation, see Bosl, *Handbuch* 2: 163–67. David Gans, *Zemah David* 2: 401, describes Maximilian's coronation in the city of "Frankfurt" (am Main) in 5322 (1562) without mentioning a ceremony in Prague.

Various outbreaks of pestilence *(pestis)* occurred throughout Europe in the last half of the sixteenth century, including the 1560s. See A. Hirsch, *Handbuch der historisch-geographischen Pathologie* (Stuttgart, 1881) 1: 352–53, where he mentions an epidemic in 1562, the year cited in the Prague chronicle, albeit in Italy. See also ibid., 1: 6, 31.

58.  This information is found in *Zemah David* 2: 405, but without specification of the day or month. "His wife, the empress, Madam Maria," was Charles V's daughter, hence Maximilian's cousin.

# [Fol. 10v]

**Regensburg** in Bavaria. **[on the appointed day]** These words appear next to the word emperor as a marginal notation, perhaps by a later hand.

[59]  5336 [1576] – Emperor Maximilian and his son King Rudolf came to Prague, along with [the emperor's] other sons. And they crowned Rudolf, may he be exalted, on the 1st of Nisan [1 March]. Afterwards, the emperor travelled to Regensburg [on the appointed day], while King Rudolf remained in Prague. The king subsequently followed his father to Regensburg, becoming [Holy Roman] Emperor there during his father's lifetime.

# [Fol. 11r]

**Old Town** *Staré Město*, or *Altstadt* in German.

[60]  5337 [1576] – In Marḥeshvan [September/October], Emperor Maximilian died in the city of Regensburg. His [body] was brought to Prague in [the month] of Adar I [January/February 1577], and left in the St. Jakob Cloister in the Old Town for six weeks until the interment.

**castle** Hradčany castle.

[61]  5337 [1577] – On Friday, the 4th of Nisan [22 March], Emperor Maximilian, may he have peace, was buried with great pomp. There were lords, dukes, envoys, monks,

---

59.  In 1575, Emperor Maximilian II and his son Rudolf came to Prague, where Rudolf was crowned king of Bohemia on 12 March 1575. See Bibl, *Maximilian II*, 383–85; G. von Schwarzenfeld, *Rudolf II, der saturmsche Kaiser* (Munich, 1961), 35–40. This event is also noted in *Ẓemaḥ David* 2: 408. A year later, in May 1576, Rudolf II was crowned Holy Roman Emperor during his father's lifetime, holding this title until 1611. See von Schwarzenfeld, *Rudolf II*, 40–41.
60.  Emperor Maximilian II died on 21 October 1576 (the beginning of 5337) in Regensburg. See Bibl, *Maximilian II*, 395–98. His death is noted in *Ẓemaḥ David* 2: 408, but is reported inaccurately as occurring in 5336. The body lay in state in the St. Jakob Cloister in the Old Town *(Staré Město)*. On this monastery, see J. M. Schottky, *Prag wie es war, und wie es ist* (Prague, 1830) 1: 277–80.
61.  This is a colorful description of the interment of Emperor Maximilian, which took place in Prague several months after his death. The royal funeral was held on 20 March 1577 (and not on 22 March, or the 4th of Nisan, as reported by the Prague

priests, and archbishops from all the lands. Preceding the coffin twenty-one flags bearing the seals of the lands under his dominion were carried, followed by twenty-one horses with fancy trappings that had been ridden by [the emperor]. And they bore three crowns—of Bohemia, Hungary, and the Holy Roman Empire—and other royal accoutrements and appurtenances. Such glory and might had not been seen or heard of since the days of Emperor Charles, of blessed memory, not even in his lifetime. There was great disorder in Prague when they bore the emperor, of blessed memory, to the castle, and no man had any spirit left [Josh. 2:11]. Great fear fell upon the Jews, and God, Blessed be He, delivered them from evil at their hands.

[62]  5337 [1577] – Grain was very cheap in Bohemia, and here in Prague, on Friday, the 6th of Av [20 July], a measure of grain called a *strich* sold for seven new [coins] and a measure of wheat for twelve.

**strich**  A measure of grain in Bohemia, Saxony, and Silesia.

## [Fol. IIv]

[63]  5337 [1577] – On the second night of Passover [3 April], in the second hour, there was a [lunar] eclipse for nearly two hours, and [the moon] was covered, and there was darkness, and within [the darkness] a bit of light.

The author inserted an illustration of the eclipse showing the extent to which the moon was covered.

chronicle). The coffin was borne from the St. Jakob Cloister in the Old Town to "the castle," the Hradčany, and interred in the cathedral of St. Vitus, the burial site of Maximilian's predecessors. See von Schwarzenfeld, *Rudolf II*, 44ff. Regarding the Hradčany, see Schottky, *Prag wie es war* 2: 86ff.

62–63. ——

The author inserted an illustration of a comet with its tail as it appeared among the other stars. This comet was observed by the Danish astronomer Tycho Brahe.

[64] 5338 [1577] – On Monday night, the 2nd of Kislev [11 November], in the second hour, a star stood out among the other stars in the east, much larger than the other stars, with a long tail, appearing thus, and shining as brightly as the moon. It remained thus for the entire month of Kislev [November/December] until the 8th of Tevet [18 December], diminishing from the middle of Kislev until its tail was very small, disappearing entirely on the 8th of Tevet. May God regard it for good and a blessing, Amen. Its like had not been seen for over forty-five years.

## [Fol. 12v]

**Hartscheurer** perhaps a type of soldier, or derived from a placename.
**Innsbruck** in Austria.
**Genova** in Italy.

[65] 5341 [1581] – On the 4th of Av [4 July], the Empress Madam Maria, and her son Duke Herzog [*sic*] Ernst, may he be exalted, and her daughter the queen of France left Prague, travelling in a large cortege [numbering] more than four hundred people. And her son Rudolf, may he be exalted, commanded that she be escorted to Vienna by two hundred mounted men, called *Hartscheurer,* from his castle. Her son Herzog Ernst, and her daughter, queen of France, remained in Vienna, while the people of Vienna accompanied [Maria] with two hundred men till Innsbruck, and

64. ———
65. The persons mentioned are (a) "the Empress Madam Maria" (1528–1603), wife of Maximilian II, daughter of Charles V, and mother of Rudolf II; (b) "her son Duke Herzog Ernst" (1553–1595); (c) "her daughter the queen of France"—Elizabeth, the wife of Charles IX of France; and (d) "Duke Ferdinand of Innsbruck"—Archduke of Tyrol (1529–1595), the son of Emperor Ferdinand I.

Duke Ferdinand of Innsbruck requisitioned an escort for her to Venice, from whence she journeyed to Genova, and from there to Spain.

[66] 5358 [1598] — On Thursday, the 4th of Adar II [12 March], the waters prevailed here in Prague, rising from gate to gate, and they could not pray in the Altneuschul, or in the Pinkasschul, and the waters remained for an entire day and night.

**Altneuschul, Pinkasschul** two of the Prague synagogues.

[67] In the same year, on Monday the 15th of Av [17 August], the waters prevailed a second time here in Prague, flooding the entire length and breadth of the Judenstraße, and people went about in a boat. They could not pray in any of the synagogues, with the exception of the Hochschul and the Klaus. The waters were more than one and a half cubits higher than the previous flood, causing great damage in Prague and the cities of Bohemia, remaining for two and a half days.

**boat** The author used the German word *Schiff.* **Klaus** *Beth Midrash,* or study house.

66. The inundation of Prague in March 1598 caused the flooding of two of its synagogues: the ancient Altneuschul, founded in 1270 (see Z. Muenzer, "Die Altneusynagoge in Prag," *Jahrbuch der Gesellschaft für Geschichte der Juden in der Cechoslovakischen Republik* 4 [1932]: 63–105); and the Pinkasschul, founded in 1535 by the Horowitz family in honor of their relative Israel Pinkas. See H. Volavkova, *The Pinkas Synagogue* (Prague, 1955).

67. The Hochschul burned down the conflagration in the Judenstraße in 1559 (see *Chronicle,* no. 53). It was rebuilt subsequently by the philanthropist R. Mordecai Meisel. See *Zemah David* 1: 146. For a summary of the existing literature concerning Meisel, see Baron, *Social and Religious History* 14: 366 nn. 16, 17. The Klaus (the Prague study house), apparently built during the reign of Maximilian II (1564–1576) by Mordecai Meisel, was where the MaHaRaL taught his disciples. See A. Gottesdiener, "Ha-Ari she-be-Hakhmey Prag," *Azkkarah le-nishmat ha-Rav . . . Kook, Qoveṣ Torani Madai* 3–4 (1937): 277–78.

## [Fol. 13r]

[68] The year 5362 [1602] was a time of trial and tribulation for the Jews here in Prague, for [they] were threatened with expulsion. The townspeople, who were the main [instigators], proposed to present the emperor, may he be exalted, with a yearly sum of several thousands [collected] from the merchants and the rest of the local populace. Several times [the Emperor] ordered that the writs of privilege be deposited in his chamber, and we were very fearful that perhaps, Heaven forbid, they would be rescinded. The emperor, may he be exalted, nearly acceded to [our enemies]; we repented greatly, for God, Blessed be He, had mercy on us, and turned from His wrath, and we were left unharmed.

68. Rudolf II displayed a favorable attitude toward the Jews upon his accession to the throne in 1576. See Bondy and Dworsky, *Zur Geschichte der Juden* 1: 550–820, nos. 760–1040; T. Jakobowitz, "Die Jüdischen Zünfte," 63–68; Baron, *Social and Religious History* 14: 162–71, 365–68.

On 14 February 1577 Rudolf renewed the writs of privilege granted to the Jews by King Wladislaw in 1510, even augmenting Jewish rights. See Bondy and Dworsky, *Zur Geschichte der Juden* 1: 554–55, no. 766. Regarding the renewal of the writs from 1593–1598, see Baron, *Social and Religious History* 14: 365–66 n. 16. The Prague chronicle relates that the Jews of Prague were in danger of expulsion in 1602 when the "townspeople" tried to bribe the emperor into rescinding the privileges he had granted to the Jews. In a document dated 1 April 1602, we find harsh accusations against the Jews brought by the governor of the Old Town of Prague and his town council in an attempt to pressure Rudolf into ordering their expulsion from Bohemia. See Bondy and Dworsky, *Zur Geschichte der Juden* 1: 770–77, no. 979. The king did not accede to their demands and continued to regard the Jews as an aid to the economic development of his country.

The emperor's "chamber" refers to the seat of the empire, which Rudolf transferred to Prague in the early years of his reign. See von Schwarzenfeld, *Rudolf II*, 41; R. J. W. Evans, *Rudolf II and his World* (Oxford, 1973), 22.

[69] During that year [1602], due to our iniquities, slanderous talebearers from among our people, one Shimmel, a servant, and Moses Trantik, of accursed memory, informed the authorities that the heads of the community were responsible for the death of Eli[jah] Pollak, and [as a result] R. Israel

## [Fol. 13v]

Henlig [Henlisch], the head of the *kehillah,* and Primaz, and Abraham Schikler were arrested and bound, and brought to Bürglitz castle, each one separately. Subsequently, on the Sabbath, the 9th of Av [27 July], they arrested the renowned luminary, the learned rabbinical authority, our teacher Rabbi Loew, may God protect and preserve him, and Manisch Schick, head of the *kehillah,* and R. Ḥayyim Wahl, head of the *kehillah,* putting them under arrest in

**kehillah** the Jewish community.

---

69–70. In these two paragraphs the story unfolds of a scandalous affair of triple denunciation that rocked the Prague Jewish community in 1602, exposing it yet again to the danger of expulsion. Two Jews, Shimon Leib ("Shimmel") and "Moses Trantik," "informed the authorities that the heads of the community were responsible for the death of Eli[jah] Pollak." The heads of the Jewish community immediately were placed under arrest in Bürglitz castle, in the Rathaus in the Old Town (mentioned again in the *Chronicle,* no. 70). See Schottky, *Prag wie es war* 1: 181–91. The communal leaders at the time were "Israel Henlisch," "Primaz," "Abraham Schikler," "the renowned luminary, the learned rabbinical authority, our teacher, R. Loew," none other than the MaHaRaL, the dominant Jewish scholar of his day, as well as "Manisch Schick," and "Ḥayyim Wahl." The synagogues remained sealed by the authorities for more than four weeks. Finally, based on testimony of "both Jews and Christians," the informers were arrested. "Shimon Leib" died in jail, while "Moses Trantik" was permanently exiled from Prague (a distance of at least "seven parasangs" [approx. 28 miles]) by official decree. The author notes here that the final detail was taken from the *pinkas* of the Prague Jewish community. Apparently he relied on the *pinkas* as a source for his accounts of other events but without specific citation (see introduction).

This *pinkas* is apparently no longer extant; in any case its location is unknown.

**Rathaus**   the town hall.
**Shemini Azeret**   the holi-
day immediately following
Sukkot.

the *Rathaus*. On Monday, the 11th of Av [29
July], all the synagogues here in Prague
were closed and sealed, and [the Jews]
were unable to pray in any synagogue for
more than four weeks. And others were
arrested in order to testify regarding the
aforementioned matter. [Days] of repentance and fasting were decreed in all the
communities of Israel, and two days of
Yom Kippur were observed here, until
God, Blessed be He, had mercy on us. At
great expense, and after much intercession,
the [prisoners] were released on bail for a
large sum. Then these two informers of
accursed memory told the authorities that
R. Israel Henlisch had requested that they
poison a non-Jew named Nikolas Preiss,
and they arrested R. I[srael] on *Shemini
Azeret* [7 October].

[70]  5363 [1602] – Three days later, he was severely castigated and tortured twice regarding this matter [of poisoning], and the
other aforementioned matters, until he
died. But God, Blessed be He, was with

It is mentioned in a seventeenth century Hebrew source entitled *Tikkun Sofrim*
containing the protocols, rulings *(takkanot)*, and notarized documents *(shetarot)*
issued by the Prague Jewish court *(bet din)* in 1640, as copied from the *pinkas* of
the Prague Jewish community. (MS Oxford-Bodleian 2230 [Opp. 615]; Institute of
Microfilmed Hebrew Manuscripts no. 20513.)

This affair is not mentioned explicitly in other sources, although some accounts
may contain oblique references. The Jews of Prague attempted to obtain the
release of their communal leaders by propitiating the authorities, as stated by the
Prague chronicler: "at great expense and after much intercession." In order to
raise the necessary funds, the Prague Jews turned to other Jewish communities.
This may be the background to a request for funds in 1603 by a delegation of two
Jews from Prague to a synod of German rabbis in Frankfurt. See E. Zimmer, *Jewish
Synods in Germany during the Late Middle Ages (1286–1603)* (New York, 1978),
89–90. Another allusion is found in an early seventeenth century Yiddish account
of exorcism of ghosts from Prague which mentions "Trantsig of Prague . . . who
was an informer," none other than the Moses Trantik of our chronicle. See

him, and he withstood the torture, making
no confession. And it came to pass that the
two informers were arrested, and both
Jews and Christians testified that they de-
served [to be sentenced] to death. And
they were taken

[Fol. 14r]

to the castle under arrest. They were imprisoned there for more than half a year;
then they were taken to the *Rathaus* [in the
Old Town]. During the period of their first
imprisonment [in the castle], they were
castigated and tortured, but they remained
intractable nonetheless, sending evil mis-
sives about the [Jewish] community and
God's people to the emperor's chamber,
may he be exalted, and to other lords, making evil accusations against the Jews, [the
likes of which] had not been heard from
the day the land was founded [Exod. 9:18],
and which cannot be recorded explicitly.
And we were terror-stricken, [living in]

S. Zfatman-Biller, "Exorcisms in Prague in the 17th Century: The Question of the
Historical Authenticity of a Folk Genre" (Hebrew), *Jerusalem Studies in Jewish
Folklore* 3 (June 1982): 22–25, 29.

The detailed description in the chronicle sheds light on the little-known history
of the Prague Jewish community in the early seventeenth century. From the
account of this affair we learn of conflicts of unclear background within the Jewish
community, as well as the composition of the Jewish leadership. The outstanding
figure in the Jewish community was the MaHaRaL, whose arrest is not known
from any other source. "Israel Henlisch" is R. Israel Henliz of the community of
Prague, mentioned in a letter sent from Jerusalem (1622) by R. Isaiah Horowitz
ha-Levi (ha-Shelah ha-Kadosh). See A. Yaari, *Letters from the Land of Israel*
(Hebrew; 2d ed., Ramat Gan, 1971), 216, where R. Isaiah also mentions his
brother R. N[. . .], of the community of Frankfurt. "Manisch Schick" is Menaḥem
Manisch Schick b. R. Abraham, who served as the head of the Prague Jewish
community for more than forty years, and who tried, unsuccessfully, to reach Erez
Israel shortly before his death. He died in Vienna on the 22nd of Tishri 5373

fear of expulsion, Heaven forbid, and other evils, if it had not been for God's help, and our master the emperor, may he be exalted, who had mercy on us. During this time, Shimon Leib, of accursed memory, died in prison and was buried where dead dogs and other carcasses are thrown by the hangman. And Moses Trantik secured his release from jail by bribery and intercession, but he had to swear that he would never enter Prague, but stay seven parasangs from there, as recorded in the minutes book of the Prague [Jewish] community.

## [Fol. 15r]

[71]   5367 [1607] – On Thursday, the 17th of Tammuz [12 July], a delegation from the Persian king arrived here in Prague, and was received with pomp and ceremony. It passed through all the local streets, including the Judenstraße, accompanied by members of the royal court. A previous delegation from this king had visited [Prague] two years earlier.

---

(1612). See the inscription on his tombstone in B. Wachstein, *Die Inschriften des alten Judenfriedhofes in Wien* (Vienna and Leipzig, 1912) 1: 48–49. His son (d. 1620) was one of the heads of the Viennese Jewish community. See Wachstein, 80–81; S. Hock, *Die Familien Prags, nach den Epitaphien des alten Jüdischen Friedhofs in Prag* (Pressburg, 1892), 362. Ḥayyim Wahl died in Prague on the 4th or the 20th of Adar I 5391 (1631), at the age of seventy-five. See Lieben, *Gal-ed*, 71, no. 139.

71.   Two delegations from Shah Abbas I of Persia visited Prague in 1604 and 1607, respectively. The emperor and the shah cooperated in their struggle against their common enemy—the Ottoman sultan. See Evans, *Rudolf II*, 77–78.

[72] 5368 [1608] – On Rosh Ḥodesh Iyyar [17 April 1608] there was contention and commotion here in Prague between our ruler Emperor Rudolf, may he be exalted, and his brother [ . . . ] Duke Matthias [ . . . ] who came to a city near Prague, residing in the city of Böhmisch Brod. With him there were great numbers of brave men mounted on steeds [Esther 8:10, 14] and armed infantry from the [ranks of the] warriors [Num. 31:49] of the countries of Austria, Moravia, Hungary, and Tatry. They did great damage to this city, stealing, rampaging, killing, and burning—inflicting damage of more than four times one hundred thousand. Duke Matthias desired to rule over the countries of Bohemia, Hungary, Moravia, and Austria by force. Our ruler, the emperor, may he be exalted, also gathered a great force from the cities of Bohemia, and a force of about twenty thousand brave armed soldiers came here, to Prague. And we were extremely disturbed. The town council posted guards in the Judenstraße to make certain

**Tatry** the Tatry mountains in the Carpathians, on the border between Czechoslovakia and Poland.

---

72.  The rivalry between Rudolf and Matthias for the crown actively erupted in the spring of 1608 ("Rosh Ḥodesh Iyyar") when Matthias's forces occupied the city of Böhmisch Brod, near Prague. On 25 June 1608, the brothers finally reached a compromise regarding the division of the eastern sector of the empire. According to this agreement, Hungary, Moravia, and Austria were to be ruled by Matthias, while Rudolf would retain dominion over Bohemia. See von Schwarzenfeld, *Rudolf II*, 224–31; Bosl, *Handbuch* 2: 189. This compromise did not end the Habsburg brothers' conflict, however (see *Chronicle*, no. 76). The chronicler stresses that the Jews remained unharmed during these disturbances, due to the posting of special guards in the Judenstraße.

## [Fol. 15v]

no Jew was harmed. This [state of affairs] lasted for about four weeks, and God, Blessed be He, delivered us from their hands. And they reached a compromise—Matthias was granted the royal crown of Hungary, [and it was agreed] that he would rule Hungary, Moravia, and Austria. After the death of our sovereign, may he be exalted, Matthias would rule over Bohemia as well. And they went peacefully on their way to Vienna, and the people of Bohemia returned to their homes.

[73] 5369 [1609] – There were severe disturbances here in Prague in conjunction with the request for a [royal] mandate from our sovereign the emperor, may he be exalted, granting the right for each man to choose his [religious] beliefs as he sees fit. And three [leaders] conspired with other lords, squires, and local rulers in all the cities of Bohemia, gathering a multitude prepared for war; and from the other lands [came] mounted soldiers and infantry [numbering] more than twenty thousand [men].

---

73. Shortly after the signing of the agreement concerning control over the eastern part of the empire, Rudolf II's position in Bohemia was undermined further by demands from Protestant sects in Bohemia, led by Wenzel Budowets, to grant them religious freedom. In 1609, Rudolf II was forced to grant the dissident sects freedom of worship, with the exception of the Pikarden sect. This anti-Catholic sect, closely related doctrinally to the Taborites, already active in Bohemia and Moravia in the fourteenth century, continued to exist for centuries. See J. Loserth, "Die Stände Mährens und die protestantischen Stände Österreichs ob und unter der Enns in der zweiten Hälfte des Jahres 1608," *Zeitschrift des deutschen Vereins für die Geschichte Mährens und Schlesiens* 4 (1900): 226–78; von Schwarzenfeld, *Rudolf II,* 231ff; Bosl, *Handbuch* 2: 189–92. On the Pikarden, see F. G. Heymann, *John Zizka and the Hussite Revolution* (Princeton, 1955), 209ff, 245ff. Concerning the "Rathaus in the New Town," see Schottky, *Prag wie es war* 1: 384–87.

They placed guards in all the streets [of Prague] and established their headquarters in the *Rathaus* in the New Town, and then in the Old Town, until [the emperor] was forced to compromise, and granted them permission to [uphold] the principles of the faith of Luther, and to build their houses of worship, and [to live according to] what they already believed, but not [to follow] the faith of the Pikarden, or other new beliefs.

**New Town**   *Nové Měste,* or *Neustadt* in German. This quarter already existed in the fourteenth century, during the reign of Charles IV.
**Old Town**   See note at no. 60, above.

## [Fol. 16r]

[74]   In the year 5370 [1609], on the eve of Sukkot [12 October], an emissary arrived from the Ottoman sultan, accompanied by approximately one hundred and twenty men, bearing generous gifts from the sultan to our sovereign, may he be exalted, worth more than one hundred and fifty thousand horses, and [ . . . ], and one tent, as well as other unusual contraptions, and they were received with lavish pomp and ceremony.

[75]   In the year 5370 [1610], an important meeting, called the *Reichstag,* was convened here in Prague. The first to arrive were the duke of Moravia named Korpirs of Sachsen with his brother, and the archbishop of Köln, and the head archbishop

---

74.   This delegation arrived approximately three years following the signing of the treaty of Zsitva Torok between Emperor Rudolf II and the Ottoman sultan Ahmed I on 11 November 1606. Regarding this treaty, see the general discussion in S. Shaw, *History of the Ottoman Empire and Modern Turkey* (Cambridge, 1976) 1: 187–88.

75.   A *Reichstag* was convened in Prague in April 1610. Attended by dukes and clergy residing in the Holy Roman Empire, its purpose was to reach a compromise between the rival brothers, Rudolf and Matthias, which it achieved. See von Schwarzenfeld, *Rudolf II,* 242.

**Koblenz** The Hebrew reads "Akloblenz." Koblenz is a suggested emendation.

**one hundred and fifty thousand** The monetary unit is not specified in the chronicle. —Trans.

of Mainz—archduke of Koblenz, our sovereign's, may he be exalted, brother, and the bishop of Passau named Leopold, duke of Steiermark, the duke of Braunschweig, and two brothers, counts of Hessen [ . . . ] and other [ . . . ] and delegates from other duchies in all parts of the Holy Roman Empire. The expenses were paid by our sovereign, may he be exalted, [ . . . ] as well as everything else, costing him more than one hundred and fifty thousand. Subsequently, a delegation to King Matthias left for Vienna, [consisting of] the archbishop of Köln, the duke of Braunschweig, and the bishop of Passau, and they negotiated an agreement between our sovereign

## [Fol. 16v]

and his brother King Matthias, may he be exalted, regarding questions of sovereignty and other issues; they issued several decrees and [settled] matters regarding [sovereignty] in the empire and other disputes. Later, each one returned safely to his home, and no one knows what the agreements were; everything was kept secret between them.

The remainder of fol. 16v was originally blank. One of the owners appended information from his time, which appears as nos. 80–81 below.

## [Fol. 17r]

[76] 5371 [1611] – There was strife and fierce fighting here in Prague for our sovereign, the emperor, may he be exalted, wanted to

---

76. The author describes in great detail the course of the bloody struggle known as the *Passaukriegsvolkes*. The background to this conflict, which led to armed strife in the streets of Prague in early 1611 between the people of Passau (Bavaria), followers of

have his cousin Leopold, bishop of Passau,
rule after his death, and Duke Grotius of
Steiermark on the throne of Bohemia. This
[conspiracy] was known only to a few, and
everything was done in utmost secrecy.
Bishop Leopold gathered a multitude,
men of war by the thousands, approximately sixteen thousand chosen men, sta-
tioning them in the city of Passau for a
year. And they did great damage there and
in the surrounding area, and no one knew
why they were in Passau. And the people
returned [to their homes] for there was
nothing to eat or drink there, for they had

---

Bishop Leopold, and the Bohemians in Prague, lies in the struggle between Rudolf and
Matthias for the Bohemian crown beginning in 1608 (see *Chronicle,* no. 72). Deliber-
ately disregarding their prior agreement (ibid.), Rudolf II attempted to crown his
relative Leopold king of Bohemia, instead of allowing Matthias, who already ruled
Hungary, Moravia, and Austria, to succeed him. The conflict lasted for several
months, with Leopold's forces gaining control of sections of Bohemia, including parts
of Prague. Matthias's army succeeded, however, in overcoming Leopold's forces.
Matthias was crowned King of Bohemia on 23 May 1611 (as reported accurately in the
chronicle, the 11th of Sivan 5371), while Rudolf II continued to occupy the throne of
the Holy Roman Empire. See F. Kurz, *Der Einfall des von Kaiser Rudolf II, in Passau
angeworbenen Kriegsvolks in ober Österreich und Böhmen (1610–1611)* (Linz,
1897); A. Chroust, *Von Einfall des Passauer Kreigsvolks bis zum nürnberger Kurfürstentag* (Munich, 1903); von Schwarzenfeld, *Rudolf II,* 243–50. The chronicle describes the invasion of Bohemia by Leopold's forces, stressing that they inflicted grave
damage on the residents of Budweis, which the chronicler interprets as divine retribu-
tion: "And [thus] God avenged the blood of his servants spilled in the decree of
Budweis in 5266 [the end of 1505]." (See *Chronicle,* no. 12.) As an eyewitness to the
events, the author of the Prague chronicle describes them at length. He recounts the
destruction of four monasteries and the murder of their residents in the storm of battle.
Two of these monasteries were located in the New Town; the Matkasvata Cloister, and
the Naslovanech Cloister, founded in the mid-fourteenth century by Charles IV. See
V. Volavaka, *Praha* (Prague, 1948), 249. The third monastery, the Nasfrantisku, was a
Franciscan monastery in the Old Town founded in the same period, or earlier; see
Volavaka, *Praha,* 198. The fourth monastery may be the Stroh Hof. (My thanks to Dr.
Avigdor Dagan for the information concerning the latter two monasteries.) The chronicler stresses that the Jews of Prague were in grave danger on three occasions, but
were saved due to the protection of the emperor: [O]ur sovereign, may he be exalted,
. . . ordered that no harm or injury be inflicted on the Jews. He guarded them as the

**classes** The author uses
the German word *Stände*.

consumed everything [ . . . ]. From there
they went to Bohemia, attacking the city of
Budweis treacherously and with trickery,
doing great damage—stealing, rampaging,
taking money, gold, and silver worth approximately a hundred thousand, and killing many of the townspeople. And [thus]
God avenged the blood of his servants
spilled in the decree of Budweis, in 5266
[the end of 1505]. Wherever they went in
Bohemia, they did great damage. When
the news reached the people of Bohemia,
the three classes—the lords, the squires,
and the local rulers—quickly gathered a
multitude of about ten thousand [men]
including the townspeople, all soldiers,
[both] mounted [men] and infantry, each
with his sword on thigh [Exod. 32:27], and
other destructive weapons of war, firearms

---

pupil of his eye." The chronicler adds that the Jews of Prague played a role in their
own defense, patrolling the Jewish quarter armed with weapons. "And the Jews
fortified the Judenstraße, closing all the gates, no one could leave or enter through the
gates. The streets with synagogues were guarded by soldiers . . . with weapons and
armor purchased at great cost at communal expense, and even the Jews bore weapons, guarding by day and by night." Furthermore, he stresses that "even on the
Sabbath, [the Jews] bore weapons." This data regarding armed self-defense by the
Jews of Prague alongside the local militia is reflected in royal documents as well. Cf.
Bondy and Dworsky, *Zur Geschichte der Juden* 1: 432, 479, 508, 550; Stein, *Die
Geschichte der Juden in Böhmen*, 58. Apparently this phenomenon of Jews bearing
arms in self-defense was not unknown, despite the various ordinances dating from as
early as the thirteenth century forbidding Jews to bear weapons. See G. Kisch, *The
Jews in Medieval Germany*, 2d ed. (New York, 1970), 111–28. For a partial compila-
tion of sources relating to the bearing of arms by Jews in medieval and modern times,
see F. Z. Cahana, "Military Service as Reflected in Responsa Literature" (Hebrew),
*Meḥqarim be-Sifrut ha-Teshuvot* (Jerusalem, 1973), 163–94.

## [Fol. 17v]

called *Büchsen* in German. On Tuesday, the 2nd of Adar [15 February 1611], at dawn, the people of Passau, numbering approximately six and a half thousand, came in full force, and broke the outer gate, and hurried to the small [quarter] called Kleinseite, killing the guards and burning our houses. And the people of Prague hurried, rising as one to oppose them. About five thousand [men] did battle with them while the remainder of the people guarded the citadel and the Hradcin as well as the Old and New Towns. Casualties fell on both sides for approximately three hours in the fighting for the outer gate and the Kleinseite. Some eight hundred or more of the residents of the Kleinseite were in league with the Passauers and fired their rifles, and poured tar and hot water from the windows onto the Bohemians, killing many. If it had not been for this [conspiracy], none of the Passauers would have had a foothold [in Prague]. The Bohemians retreated to the Old Town, closing the gate to the bridge, guarding this place so no one could leave or [enter—Josh. 6:1] the Kleinseite for the New Town. And the Passauers prepared to attack the outer gate and the Kleinseite, and [ . . . ] behind the citadel. They placed a large cannon,

## [Fol. 18r]

a weapon of destruction, opposite these places, intending to destroy them, especially the Judenstraße. All this was done without the knowledge of our sovereign,

**Büchsen**   rifles.

**outer gate**   *ausse.* This probably refers to the outer edge of the city.

**Kleinseite**   The small quarter west of the Voltava River known also as Malá Strana, which was joined to the Old Town by a bridge.

**citadel**   apparently the Wysschrad.

**Hradcin**   Hradcin (or Hradčany) is the name of a fortress built in the second half of the ninth century. —Trans.

**bridge**   over the Voltava River connecting the Old Town to the Kleinseite, built by Charles IV in 1357.

**large cannon**   *gross Geschütz* is the German term used by the author.

the emperor, may he be exalted. When this was made known to our sovereign, may he be exalted, he immediately ordered that the cannon be returned to their place, that no damage be done to those places, and [specifically] ordered that no harm or injury should be inflicted on the Jews. [He] guarded them as the pupil of his eye [Deut. 32:10], for the Passauers intended to destroy, rob, and take spoils, Heaven forbid, and God, Blessed be He, saved us from them. And the Jews fortified the Judenstraße, closing all the gates; no one could leave or enter through the gates. The streets with synagogues were guarded by soldiers under the lead command of the Graf [Count] of Tonia, [who guarded the Jews] like any other nation, with weapons and armor purchased at great cost at communal expense, and even the Jews bore weapons, guarding by day and by night. Even on the Sabbath, [the Jews] bore weapons.

## [Fol. 18v]

I shall recount another miracle as great as the Exodus from Egypt and the splitting of the Red Sea. On the aforementioned day, on Tuesday, in the first hour after midday, the masses arose by the thousands and destroyed four monasteries here in Prague. First [they destroyed] the Matkasvata Cloister in the New Town, built in the New Town from [a sum] of several thousands donated by the emperor's mother before her death. It housed monks who walked barefoot, without shoes. Of the

**emperor's mother** Maria, the mother of Rudolf, and daughter of Charles V, d. 1603. See no. 65.
**barefoot** known as the *Barfüßer.*

fourteen monks there, not one survived. And they stole and rampaged, [taking] everything they found and destroying the chapel and [the monks'] residence. They destroyed everything totally. There was a dead prince called Ferdinand of Dany in his coffin, whom they removed from his grave, stripping him of his clothing, silk clothes called *sammt*. [In order] to remove a valuable diamond ring, they amputated his finger with the ring. At the Naslovenach Cloister, they killed the abbot. At the Stroh Hof, and in the Old Town, at the Nasfrantisku Cloister, they looted and wreaked havoc and destruction. Afterwards, they intended to harm the Jews as well—to massacre and exterminate [Esther 3:13]

**Ferdinand of Dany** unknown to us.
**removed from his grave** The corpses of kings and lords were embalmed before being buried in this monastery. On embalming, see no. 78 below.
**sammt** velvet.
**Stroh Hof** This identification is not definite.
**Nasfrantisku Cloister** a Franciscan monastery.

## [Fol. 19r]

all the Jews, to rob and plunder all their money, Heaven forbid!—if it had not been for the mercy of the Lord of Hosts, who sent an angel into the midst of the crowd, and they heard a voice [proclaiming], "Do not raise your hands against the Jews, by order of our sovereign the emperor, may he be exalted." The lords, the leaders of the people, came to the aid of the Jews, for [the masses] had no right to harm the Jews. We were terror-stricken, [being at the mercy] of the masses on the one hand, and of the Passauers on the other, who also, Heaven forbid, intended to rob and plunder [the Jews]. We repented greatly, prayed, and performed works of charity, declaring a public fast-day, and praying in

**repented greatly, prayed, and performed works of charity** This formula appears in the liturgy for the Day of Atonement. —Trans.

the synagogue all night long; for two days we fasted and sought pardon for our sins. At this time, the Bohemians sent [messengers] to Vienna, asking King Matthias for help, and he sent the Bohemians nine thousand brave mounted soldiers and armed infantry, later arriving in person accompanied by four thousand soldiers and nobles. On Thursday, the 10th of Nisan [24 March 1611], he was received with great honors, taking up residence in the Old Town, in the aforementioned [ . . . ], later moving to the Hradcin castle in the house of [ . . . ]. When Leopold, [along with] his lords, advisors, and the Passauers, saw

## [Fol. 19v]

that the Bohemians had gathered a multitude from all the cities of Bohemia, and that Matthias's followers supported them, Leopold and his supporters fled at night without the knowledge of the Bohemians, coming to the city of Budweis. In the morning, when the Bohemians gave pursuit, they were unable to overtake them, and returned to Prague. Afterwards there was a conclave in the citadel, but they could not reach an agreement regarding the monarchy, and there was discord and controversy between them until a compromise was reached between our sovereign the emperor, may he be exalted, and his brother Matthias of Bohemia, as is well known but cannot be recorded. On Monday, the 11th of Sivan 5371 [23 May 1611], our sovereign Matthias was crowned king of all the cities of Bohemia and Silesia with great pomp and ceremony. And we, the Jews, as well as the Christians, were greatly afraid of the masses and soldiers, lest they attack, rob, and plunder us, Heaven forbid, and the Christians. King Matthias himself commanded his lords and advisors to guard the Jews especially, [to ensure] that not a single one be harmed.

## [Fol. 20r]

He assigned six hundred armed soldiers from among his supporters to [guard] the Judenstraße, and the lords of Bohemia assigned several hundred men to protect and guard us as well.

[77] An event that occurred in our holy community in the year 5391, on the eighth day of Adar II [12 March 1631]—the martyrdom of a member of our community, R. Anschel Lachmanin [in] 5391. He was sentenced to execution by burning by order of the duke, who was second only to the king, with the backing of seven non-Jewish courts.

**eighth day** The Hebrew reads: the eighth day of the new moon of Adar II.

[78] An event that occurred in the same year, on Rosh Ḥodesh Tammuz [1 July]—that same duke died a strange death; that is, he had never suffered from any illness, and even a quarter of an hour prior to his death he was rejoicing with his servants, until the fifth hour of the night. [But] in the sixth hour he was taken by a strange death. After his death, he was embalmed like all kings

Not all the details recorded here are clear. Apparently the author's knowledge of Hebrew was quite poor.

---

77. The martyrdom of R. Anschel in Prague in 1631 is obscure.
78. ———

The meaning of the last lines of fol. 20r and the first line of fol. 20v is unclear.

**trees[?]** The Hebrew text reads *c'ylt* [unknown] *shebayaar* [in the forest].
—TRANS.

and princes, and on the third day while he was lying in his coffin, which was covered with pitch on the outside and plaster on the inside [ . . . ] and the body inside was anointed with a fatty whitewash,

[ . . . ]

[Fol. 20v]

[ . . . ]

[79] 5453 [1693] – On the 9th of Av [11 August], while eating the final meal before the fast, there was a strong wind and an earthquake, the likes of which had never been heard [ . . . ] and it broke several [ . . . ] and several trees[?] in the forest, and the stored grain was destroyed by this earthquake on the eve of the 9th of Av.

[Fol. 16v]

[80] 5462 [1702] – On the 15th of Shevat [13 February] a rainbow was visible in the sky.

[81] On the Sabbath, Rosh Ḥodesh Tevet 5468 [25 December 1707], the weekly portion of *Va'era* [Exod. 6:2–9:35], between the time for the afternoon prayer and the third Sabbath meal, the sky was covered with clouds, there was thunder and lightning for an entire hour, and [ . . . ] for nearly two hours. May God, Blessed be He, regard it for us and all Israel for good, [as an indication] of the end of our exile and the coming of the Messiah. Amen. Selah.

79. ——
80. ——
81. ——

The old Jewish cemetery in Prague, founded at the beginning of the fifteenth century. Several prominent Jewish personalities are buried there, and their tombstones have survived. These include: Avigdor Kara (d. 1439); Aaron Meschullam Horowitz (c. 1470–1545); Mordecai Kohen (d. 1592) and his son Bezalel (d. 1589); Mordecai Meisel (1528–1601); Jehudah ben Bezalel, called Rabbi Loew (1512–1609); David Gans (1541–1613); Joseph Delmedigo of Candia (1591–1655); and David Oppenheim (1664–1736), chief rabbi of Prague and Bohemia. (Photograph courtesy of CEDOK Czechoslovak Travel Bureau of New York.)

# Appendix 1
## Lists of Anti-Jewish Acts during the Medieval Period

### List A: Jewish Theological Seminary of America, New York, MS. Mic. 3849

[Fol. IV]

The decrees of 856 in the fifth millennium [1096], due to our iniquities. In the fifth millennium [in the year] 856.

[1] 4856 [1096]. On the 8th of Iyyar [3 May 1096], on the Sabbath, due to our iniquities there was a massacre in Speyer, and some ten [Jews] were killed. A righteous woman there took her own life.

[2] 4856 [1096]. On the 23rd of Iyyar [18 May 1096] there was a massacre in the holy community of Worms. Some of the survivors were killed in the archbishop's chamber. In the same year, on Rosh Ḥodesh Sivan [25 May 1096], [there were further attacks on Jews]. Approximately eight hundred were martyred in Worms during these two months. All were buried.

[3] 4856 [1096]. On the 3rd of Sivan [27 May 1096] there was a massacre in Mainz;

**4856** Many of the Jewish years are written without the millennium which has been added throughout without square brackets. —Trans.

1–3. These paragraphs are a concise summary of the massacres of 1096, which occurred in the course of the First Crusade, as reported by the Raban (R. Eliezer b. Nathan of Mainz). Cf. A. Neubauer and M. Stern, *Hebräische Berichte über die Judenverfolgungen während der Kreuzzüge* (Berlin, 1892) 1: 36–46. Cf. also A. M. Habermann, *Gezerot Ashkenaz ve-Ṣorfat (Anti-Jewish Acts in Ashkenaz and France;* Jerusalem, 1971), 72–82. Comparison with Joseph ha-Kohen's *Divrey ha-Yamim* reveals that no use was made of his account, which also records the major events cited by the Raban. Cf. *Divrey ha-Yamim* 1–2, fols. 12r–18v. The source of the report that the massacres of 1096 affected the Viennese *kehillah* is unknown. No similar information is found either in the account by the Raban or in the parallel chronicle composed by R. Solomon b. Samson. Cf. Neubauer and Stern, *Hebräische Berichte*, 1–31; Habermann, *Gezerot*, 24–60.

**Regensburg** in Bavaria.

**5906** should read 4906.
**Kärnten** in Austria.
**Halle** in Saxony.

**minyanim** A minyan is
the minimum number of
men, ten, required for
public prayer. —TRANS.

**Orléans** in France.

[those killed] numbered one thousand three hundred. Due to our iniquities all were killed on a single day. Many took their own lives, and some even killed their children. What happened in these *kehillot* occurred in other places as well in that year—In Vienna, Regensburg, Prague, and other large communities. I weary of their enumeration. All died in sanctification of the Name. May God avenge them!

[4]   5906 [1146]. There were many attacks on Jews and countless persons died in sanctification of the Name in the cities of the Rhineland, the Kärnten mountains, Bohemia, and Halle.

[5]   4931 [1171]. There was a massacre in the great city of Blois, in France. Those killed numbered approximately four minyanim.

[6]   4940 [1180]. Some [Jews] were killed in the cities of the Rhineland.

[7]   4950 [1190]. Some [Jews] were killed in London, among them the esteemed rabbi and teacher, R. Jacob of Orléans.

---

4–7.   These paragraphs are a concise summary of *Sefer ha-Zekhirah* (The Book of Remembrance) by R. Ephraim b. Jacob of Bonn, which recounts the attacks on Jews in Germany, France, and England during the Second and Third Crusades and the intervening period. Cf. Neubauer and Stern, *Hebräische Berichte*, 58–75; Habermann, *Gezerot*, 115–32. In paragraph 4, the author mistakenly wrote fifth instead of fourth for the millennium. Other extant sources refer to the massacre at Blois in 1171. See S. Spiegel, *"In Monte Dominus Videbitur:* The Martyrs of Blois and the Early Accusations of Ritual Murder" (Hebrew), *Mordecai M. Kaplan Jubilee Volume* (Hebrew section; New York, 1953), 263–87; L. J. Weinberger, "A New *Qinah* for the Martyrs of Blois by R. Abraham b. Samuel of Speyer" (Hebrew), *PAAJR* 44 (1977): 41–47, which also lists other published literary sources. On R. Jacob of Orléans, one of the Tosafists, see E. E. Urbach, *The Tosaphists: Their History, Writings, and Methods* (Hebrew; Jerusalem, 1980), 142–44. Kärnten and Halle are identified according to H. Tykocinski, *Germania Judaica* (Frankfurt, 1917) 1: 124–30, 140–42, and are not located in France as was mistakenly thought by Neubauer and Stern, *Hebräische Berichte*, 194.

## [Fol. 2r]

[8]  4958 [1298]. There was a massacre of Jews
in Würzburg on Wednesday, the 14th of Av
[24 July]. In that year, on the 19th of Tammuz [30 June] there was a massacre in
Kitzingen, and in Rothenburg as well,
where thirty people were killed.

[9]  865 in the fifth millennium [1105]. Rashi,
of blessed memory, died. He was called R.
Shlomo, and Shlomo Yiṣhaki by some.

[10]  931 in the fifth millennium [1171]. Rabbenu
Tam, of blessed memory, died.

[11]  249 in the sixth millennium [1488]. The
Markgraf and the archbishop of Würzburg
expelled their Jews.

**Würzburg, Kitzingen,
Rothenburg** in the district
of Franconia, Germany.

**Markgraf** Margrave, or
duke.

8.  This entry refers to the massacres by Rindfleisch in 1298, which the author
mistakenly dated as occurring in 4958 instead of 5058. In Würzburg the Jews were
attacked on the 13th of Av, and not on the 14th as reported here. Cf. S. Salfeld, *Das
Martyrologium des nürnberger Memorbuches* (Berlin, 1898), 43–48, where the
names of the deceased martyrs are listed. In Kitzingen, the Jews were attacked on
the 19th of Tammuz; ibid., 31. In Rothenburg, the Jews were attacked on three
occasions; ibid., 39–43. The date of the initial disturbance is unknown; perhaps it
occurred on the date recorded here. The second attack was on the 8th of Av, and
the third on the 12th of Av. Hundreds died in the massacre at Rothenburg, so the
number of dead cited here may refer only to the initial attack. Regarding these
massacres, see also Bernfeld, *Sefer ha-Demaot* 2: 33–59; B. Z. Dinur, *Israel in
Exile* (Hebrew; Jerusalem, 1967), vol. 2, book 2, 594–98.

9–10.  The dates of the deaths of Rashi and his grandson, Rabbenu Tam, are also found in
a notation in a manuscript of *Siddur Rashi:* "Rashi died in the sixty-fifth year of the
ninth century of the fifth millennium, that is, in 4865 [1105] . . . and Rabbenu Tam in
the thirty-first year of the tenth century in the fifth millennium." See Urbach, *The
Tosaphists,* 111. Other Hebrew sources, too, indicate that this was indeed the year of
Rashi's death. See V. Aptowitzer, *Mavo le-Sefer Ravyah* (Jerusalem, 1938), 403 n. 4.

11.  On 6 October 1488 (the beginning of 5249), Bishop Rudolf II and the duke of
Franconia issued an edict expelling the Jews of Würzburg. This edict has been
published by S. Haenle, *Geschichte der Juden im ehomligen Fürstenthum Ansbach*
(Ansbach, 1867), 210. See also M. A. Szulwas, *Die Juden in Würzberg während des
Mittelalters* (Berlin, 1934), 82–83.

**Ispamiya**   the Mishnaic
term for Spain. E.g., *Bava
Batra* 3: 2.

[12]   253 in the sixth millennium [1493]. There
was the expulsion from Spain, which is
called Ispamiya. I heard that [Jews] had
dwelt there from the time of the destruction of the First Temple, and did not return
[to Ereẓ Israel] when the Second Temple
was being built.

[13]   5252 [1492]. The Jews in the cities of [the
duchy] of Mecklenburg were martyred.

**Steiermark**   an Austrian
duchy.
**Kärnten**   near Steiermark.

[14]   5256 [1496]. [The Jews] were expelled from
the cities of Austria, as well as from Steiermark and Kärnten.

**Salzburg**   in Austria.

[15]   5258 [1498]. There was a decree of forced
conversion in the land of Portugal, with
most [Jews], young and old, forced to convert from Judaism, mingling [with the
non-Jews]. In the same period, the [Jews]
were expelled from Salzburg.

12.   The author did not record the year accurately, writing 5253 instead of 5252 (1492).
This entry reflects a widely held tradition regarding the earliness of the Jewish
settlement in Spain in general, and in Toledo in particular. By maintaining that Jews
had settled in Spain during the First Temple period, even before the appearance of
Jesus, Spanish Jews attempted to counter claims that they bore responsibility for the
Crucifixion. This apologetic argument was based on legendary and pseudo-epigraphic
traditions. See H. Beinart, "Cuando Llegaron los Judios a España?" *Estudios* 3 (1961):
1–32; idem, "Two *Shalom al Israel* Inscriptions from Spain" (Hebrew), *Eretz Israel* 8
(E. L. Sukenik Memorial Volume, 1967): 298–304. See also David, "Historiographical
Work of Gedalya ibn Yaḥya," 107–9.

13.   In 1492, twenty-seven Mecklenburg Jews were burned at the stake, with the re-
mainder expelled from the entire duchy. See L. Donath, *Geschichte der Juden in
Mecklenburg* (Leipzig, 1874), 50–58. The martyrs' names were recorded in a *yizkor*
(memorial) list found in the memorial book of the Münden Jewish community. See
Löwenstein, "Memorbücher," 196, in which twenty-nine names are listed. However,
Löwenstein did not specify the date of the execution.

14.   Jews resided in the Austrian duchy of Steiermark from the eleventh century until their
expulsion in 1496. See A. Rosenberg, *Beiträge zur Geschichte der Juden in Steiermark*
(Leipzig, 1914), 97ff. The Jews of the adjacent Austrian duchy of Kärnten also were
expelled at this time.

15.   The decree of forced conversion in Portugal, and the ensuing expulsion of the Jews,
date from 1497–1498. See I. Tishby, *Messianism in the Time of the Expulsion from
Spain and Portugal* (Hebrew; Jerusalem, 1985).
        The Jews of Salzburg were expelled in 1498. See A. Altmann, *Geschichte der Juden
in Stadt und Land Salzburg* (Berlin, 1913) 1: 169–91.

| | |
|---|---|
| [16] 5259 [1499]. The [Jews] of Nuremberg were expelled. A year or two later, the [Jews] of Ulm [were expelled], as well as those of Schwäbisch Gmünd and Giengen. | **Nuremberg** in Franconia, Germany. **Ulm, Schwäbisch Gmünd, Giengen** in Württemberg, Germany. |
| [17] 5262 [1502]. [An expulsion from] Bopfingen. | **Bopfingen** in Württemberg. This identification is tentative. |

[Fol. 2v]

| | |
|---|---|
| [18] 5263 [1503]. The Jews of the Mark [of Brandenburg] were expelled. | |
| [19] 5266 [1506]. There were expulsions from Donauwörth, Rothenburg, and Weissenburg. | **Donauwörth** in Bavaria. **Weissenburg** in Franconia. |
| [20] 5266 [1506]. There were an expulsion from Nördlingen. | **Nördlingen** in Bavaria. |

16. The expulsion of the Jews from Ulm was carried out on 6 August 1499, only several months after the expulsion of the Jews of Nuremberg. These expulsions were noted by R. Joseph of Rosheim. See *Sefer Hammiknah*, ed. H. Fränkel-Goldschmidt (Jerusalem, 1970), 11–13, as well as Fränkel-Goldschmidt's summation in the introduction, xxi–xxv. Regarding various aspects of the social structure of the Nuremberg Jewish community shortly prior to the expulsion, see M. Toch, "The Jewish Community of Nuremberg in the Year 1489—Social and Demographic Structure" (Hebrew), *Zion* 45 (1980): 61–72. No other known documentation exists for the expulsions from Schwäbisch Gmünd and Giengen.

17. No other known documentation exists for the expulsion of the Jews from Bopfingen in 1502.

18. The Jews of this principality were expelled on 29 September 1503 (the 9th of Tishri 5264). See Heise, *Die Juden in der Mark Brandenburg*, 195ff.

19. No other known documentation exists for these expulsions in 1506. It seems that the author erred regarding the date, and in fact is referring to expulsions that occurred at a later date. The Jews of Donauwörth were expelled in 1518; see List B, par. 6. The Jews of Rothenburg were expelled at the end of 1519 or the beginning of 1520. See the summary in A. Schnizlein, "Zur Geschichte der Vertreibung der Juden aus Rothenburg O. Tauber 1519/1520," *MGWJ* 61 (1917): 263–84. The expulsion from Weissenburg occurred in 1520. See M. Stern, "Die Vertreibung der Juden aus Weissenburg 1520," *ZGJD*, n.s., 1 (1929): 297–303.

20. The Jews of Nördlingen were expelled on 27 October 1506 (the 9th of Marḥeshvan 5267). See M. Stern, "Achtenstücke zur Vertreibung der Juden aus Nördlingen," *ZGJD* 4 (1890): 87–91; L. Mueller, *Aus fünf Jahrhunderten* (Augsburg, 1900), 75–79.

[21]  5270 [1510]. There was a decree in the realm
      of Mark Brandenburg, by Markgraf Jo-
      achim.
[22]  5280 [1520]. On Purim [5 March], there was
      an expulsion from Regensburg.

---

21.  This entry refers to the accusation of Host desecration in Berlin (located in the Mark of
     Brandenburg) in 1510, which resulted in thirty-eight Jewish deaths. See my note on
     *Chronicle* no. 14. The noble mentioned here is Joachim I (1484–1535), renowned for
     his cruelty, who was the guiding spirit behind contemporary anti-Jewish acts. Joachim
     is also mentioned in Joseph of Rosheim's diary, where he is called "Markgraf Yokhvo"
     (should read Yokhin). See Kracauer, "Rabbi Joselmann de Rosheim," 92 n. 22. See also
     List B, par. h.
22.  The expulsion of the Jews from Regensburg has received extensive attention. It was
     implemented on 21 February 1519 (the 20th of Adar 5279); thus the date cited here is
     incorrect. Joseph of Rosheim included an account of the expulsion and its circum-
     stances in his diary. See Kracauer, "Rabbi Joselmann de Rosheim," 88–89; Joseph of
     Rosheim, *Sefer Hammiknah,* 14–15. For a concise summary of this topic, see Fränkel-
     Goldschmidt, *Sefer Hammiknah,* xxv–xxix, and the bibliography there.

# List B: London British Library, Add. 18684

## [Fol. 352v]

[1] In 5279 [1519], Emperor Charles, may he be exalted, was crowned. [He was] Maximilian's brother-in-law.

[2] At that time, some of the changes in the Catholic faith instituted by the priest Martin Luther in Wittenberg, in the district of Meissen, spread, until accepted by many in the cities and large towns. Nearly all the inhabitants of the region followed his laws and rules, creating rivalry between Red and Red. The final outcome cannot be predicted. I only hope this will not affect [the prophecy] "in that day there shall be one Lord [with one name" —Zech. 14:9].

**laws and rules** A biblical expression found in Deut. 11:1, Neh. 10:30, for example. —TRANS.
**Red and Red** between Christians.

[3] In the year 5265 [1505], because of a [blood] libel the Jews of Budweis sanctified the Name of God, Blessed be He. Fourteen righteous women as well were drowned in sanctification of the Name. May God avenge them with the other martyrs of Israel [ . . . ].

[4] In the year 5275 [1515] [ . . . ].

[5] In the year 5266 [1506] [the Jews] of Nördlingen were expelled. The synagogue, the cemetery, and their houses were appropriated, without compensation.

---

1. Charles V succeeded Maximilian I as Holy Roman Emperor in 1519. He was Maximilian's grandson, not his brother-in-law as mentioned here.
2. This entry refers to the birth of the Lutheran Reformation in 1519 in Wittenberg.
3. The Jews of Budweis were martyred in 5266 (December 1505), and not in 5265 as written here. See *Chronicle*, no. 12.
4. The rest of the sentence is undecipherable.
5. This event is noted laconically in List A, par. 20.

**Donauwörth**   in Bavaria.

[6]   In the year 5278 [1518], the Jews of my hometown, Donauwörth, were expelled. The day after we left town, they set upon [the Jewish neighborhood] and appropriated the houses [and the cemetery as well].

[7]   In the year 5285 [1525] the peasants began to rebel against their lords in several districts in Ashkenaz [Germany]. According to the reports, more than one hundred thousand peasants were killed. So may [all your enemies] perish, [O Lord —Judg. 5:31]. The peasants burned and destroyed churches, as well as several castles and strong estates. In Franconia, only three fortresses remained. They also intended to kill Jews or force them to convert, had it not been for the Lord, who was on our side [Psalms 124:1, 2], performing miraculous wonders equal to the parting of the Red Sea.

[8]   At the end of 5266 [1506], the Jews returned to the Mark [of Brandenburg] under the rule of Markgraf Joachim, of accursed memory. At the end of 5270 [1510], he made an accusation against [the Jews], torturing them with unheard-of se-

---

6.   This entry refers to Donauwörth, Bavaria, the writer's residence. The expulsion edict was implemented on 23 July 1518. See *Germania Judaica* (Tübingen, 1987), vol. 3, 238–39, par. 13. See also List A, part. 19.

7.   Regarding the peasant uprising, see *Chronicle*, no. 20. Various sources indicate that this rebellion against the German oligarchy affected the Jews as well, because of their unique socioeconomic status as moneylenders and creditors. The author stresses that in the course of these disturbances the Jews were exposed to the danger of being killed or being forced to convert; calamity was averted, however. A similar portrayal of the situation is found in R. Joseph of Rosheim's diary (Kracauer, "Rabbi Joselmann de Rosheim," 89), where he describes his personal intervention in this matter. For a summation of this topic, see Baron, *Social and Religious History* 13: 268–69, 449–50; S. Stern, *Josel von Rosheim* (Stuttgart, 1959), 65–71.

8.   Following their expulsion on 29 September 1503, the Jews were allowed to return to the Mark of Brandenburg. See List A, par. 18. The results of the accusation of Host desecration in this district in 1510 are well known—the "burning [of] thirty-eight . . .

verity, and burning thirty-eight pure, righteous, saintly souls, who sanctified God's Name, Blessed be He. This was on Friday, the 12th of Av [19 July 1510], the eve of *Shabbat Naḥamu*. Due to our iniquities, he took several Jews against their will, confiscating all their money [ . . . ].

**Shabbat Naḥamu** the Sabbath of Consolation following the 9th of Av when the prophetic reading begins with the words, "Comfort, oh comfort My people" (Isa. 40:1).
—Trans.

## [Fol. 353r]

[9] In the year 3828 after the creation of the world [68 C.E.], due to our iniquities the Second Temple was destroyed. May it be speedily restored in our time. Fourteen hundred twenty-five years have passed since the destruction to the present, 5253 years after the creation of the world [1493].

[10] In that year, due to our iniquities, there was the expulsion from Spain, which is Ispamiya, or Spanie[n] in German. [The Jews] had lived there until that time from the destruction of the First Temple, or even earlier. They did not return [to Ereẓ Israel] with Ezra the Scribe. Thus, they dwelt there for more than nineteen hundred years. May our father in heaven bring redemption speedily. Amen.

---

souls." See *Chronicle*, no. 14, which also cites the 12th of Av 5270 (19 July 1510) as the date of the decree.

9. The date of the destruction of the Second Temple cited here, 68 C.E., reflects the tradition found in *Seder Olam* and other sources. See A. A. Akawya, "The Chronology of the Two Temples and their Destruction" (Hebrew), *Tarbiz* 39 (1970): 349–55.

10. Many traditions assign the date of the Jewish settlement in Spain to the Second Temple period or earlier. See List A, par. 12. Both Lists A and B give the date of the expulsion as 5253; however, it was actually implemented during the last two months of 5252 (1492).

**Ödenberg**   present-day
Sopron, Hungary.
**Graz**   in Austria.

[11]   In the year 5254 [1493] Emperor Frederick died, and his son was placed on his throne. At the beginning of his reign some [members] of the Jewish communities in Austria were arrested in connection with the false denunciation of the Christians. With God's help all were released, except for one man who died in prison from the severe torture; Mulmann of Ödenburg was his name. May God avenge him. Another man by the name of Jonathan of Graz was arrested. May God, Blessed be He, remove him from darkness to light, and incline the king's heart favorably to us. May it be God's will, Amen. Written on Sunday night, the 27th of Shevat, 5254 [3 February 1494].

**mercy**   The author made a play on words here and in the previous paragraph; the Hebrew letters used to indicate the date (254) also spell the Hebrew word for *mercy*. —TRANS.

[12]   At the end of that year, due to our iniquities mercy was transformed into cruelty. There was plague in the Lord's community [Num. 27:17] of Nuremberg, and many died from the change in the air, including men of good deeds, and pious, saintly men. Children and infants who feasted on dainties lay famished in the streets [Lam. 4:5]. More than eighty died. In other Jewish communities, too, in the upper and lower regions, many settlements felt the Lord's fierce anger [Deut. 9:19]; His fury

11.   Frederick III died in 1493, and was succeeded by his son Maximilian I, mentioned in par. 1 above. Regarding persecution of the Jews in Austria during this period, see D. Herzog, *Urkunden und Regesten zur Geschichte der Juden in der Steiermark (1475–1585)* (Graz, 1934), xxiiiff., 9–12, 74–78. Other sources mention Jonathan of Graz. See *Germania Judaica*, vol. 3, 464, par. 13b, no. 6.

12.   The outbreak of plague in Nuremberg in 1494, which claimed many victims including Jews, is noted in the minutes of the town council meeting of 9 August 1494. See M. Stern and S. Salfeld, *Die israelitische Bevölkerung der deutschen Städte* (Kiel, 1894–1896), vol. 3, *Nürnberg im Mittelalter*, 310–11.

blazed like fire [Ps. 89:47]. But He, being merciful, forgave iniquity and would not destroy, and did not give full vent to His fury [Ps. 78:38]. God had mercy on the remnant of His flock to ensure our survival in our land [Gen. 45:7]. May God send the son of David, our Messiah, and rebuild Jerusalem, His holy city, His footstool [Isa. 66:1], Amen. Happy is he who faithfully awaits His redemption. I, the Lord, will speed it in due time [Isa. 60:22].

[13] At the beginning of the year 5258 [1498] rumors came of a decree of forced conversion in the land of Portugal. All, young and old, were forced to convert from Judaism, and to mingle [among the non-Jews]. May God, Blessed be He, keep us from harm, Amen.

[14] At the end of 5263 [1503] the Jews were expelled.

[15]     What shall I say and how shall I speak?
         How shall I compose words?
         For I am an object of scorn to every
             passerby,
         Submitting to blow after blow.

In the year 5258 [1498], the [Jewish] inhabitants of Salzburg were expelled. They were given two days to uproot themselves and flee. The archbishop appropriated the synagogue and the cemetery, and sold their houses.

---

13. Regarding the decree of forced conversion in Portugal, see List A, par. 15.
14. The author apparently is referring to the expulsion of the Jews from the Mark of Brandenburg noted in List A, par. 18. The expulsion actually was carried out on 29 September 1503 (the 9th of Tishri 5264).
15. No other known documentation exists for this event.

**Jubilee**  See historical
notes.

[16]  In the year 5249 [1499], there was an expulsion from Nuremberg. The town council
appropriated the synagogue and the cemetery, and all the [Jews'] houses without
compensation or payment.

[17]  In the year 5259 [1499] their protection departed from them [Num. 14:9], and the
[Jews] of Ulm were expelled, as they had
been expelled from Nuremberg. Who can
hear and remain tearless? Alas, for we have
sinned. Our synagogues and our ancestors'
graves have been plowed under, and many
rise against us to expel and destroy us,
Heaven forbid! In this year, [the fourth] in
their reckoning of the Jubilee, may the
merciful One have pity [on us . . .].

[18]  In the year 5249 [1488] the prince Markgraf
and the archbishop of Würzburg expelled
their Jews.

[19]  In the year 5252 [1492] the Jews of Mecklenburg sanctified God's name. May God
avenge them!

[20]  Some time later, in the year 5256 [1496] the
king expelled all the Jews in his dominions—in Austria, Steiermark, and Kärnten. Some went to the border [area]
between Hungary and Austria. This was

16.  On the expulsion of the Jews from Nuremberg, see List A, par. 16.
17.  On the expulsion of the Jews from Ulm in 1499, see the note to List A, par. 16. "Their
     reckoning of the Jubilee" is based on the decree of Pope Paul II (pope 1464–1471),
     which established that a Jubilee (Holy Year) be observed once in twenty-five years,
     beginning with 1470. See *New Catholic Encyclopedia* 7: 108. Thus, this expulsion
     occurred four years following the last Holy Year.
18.  List A, par. 11 contains a very similar account. See the discussion in the introduction.
19.  See List A, par. 13.
20.  See List A, par. 14. The expulsion was consonant with the policy of persecution of
     Austrian Jewry pursued by Maximilian I upon his accession to the throne of the Holy
     Roman Empire in 1493. See my comments on par. 11 above.

done with the explicit permission of King Maximilian, may he be exalted, who took money from the local populace and allowed them to expel [the Jews] and appropriate their houses, the synagogue, and the cemetery.

# Appendix 2
## Excerpts from *Ẓemaḥ David* relating to Bohemia

[1] 5149 [1389]. In Prague, men of low character gathered on Isru Ḥag, the day after Passover, 5149 [18 April 1389], and attacked the Jews with swords and woodcutter's axes, killing them in the streets and burning their houses. They even removed corpses from their graves. See the elegy composed by R. Avigdor Kara that begins *Et Kol ha-Telaaḥ* [All the hardships] in the prayerbook of the Prague Jewish community, paragraph 164 [1: 132–33].

[2] 5260 [1500]. In 5260 R. Lemlein announced the coming of the Messiah, and his tidings were widely believed throughout the diaspora. His renown spread among the non-Jews as well, and many believed his message. My master and teacher, my grandfather, Seligmann Gans of blessed memory, smashed the special oven [used only] for the baking of matzah, based on [R. Asher's] promise that next year he would bake the unleavened bread in the Holy Land. I myself, the writer, heard from my venerable teacher, R. Eliezer Trèves, the rabbi of the holy community of Frankfurt, that this was no empty gesture, for [R. Asher] gave signs, and he said that perhaps our sins delayed the coming of the Messiah [1: 137].

---

1. See Historical Notes, *Chronicle*, no. 1.
2. See Historical Notes, *Chronicle*, no. 11. On R. Eliezer Trèves of Frankfurt, see M. Horovitz, *Frankfurter Rabbinen: Ergänzungen von J. Unna* (Jerusalem, 1969), 30–36, 271–73.

[3]   5301 [1541]. There were many large con-
flagrations throughout Bohemia in [5]301
[set by] an unknown arsonist. The shep-
herds and the Jews were denounced, the
people saying, "You committed this evil."
They were tortured into admitting [deeds]
they never would have committed, and
many died in sanctification of the Name,
Blessed be He, at an auto-da-fé. For this
reason, because of the accusations of the
people, Ferdinand, king of Bohemia, expelled the Jews from the entire kingdom of
Bohemia, allowing only ten [Jewish] men
to remain in Prague temporarily. But after
a short time, within less than a year, the
king and the people discovered on whose
account this misfortune had come upon
them, and realizing that the Jews had been
accused falsely, spoke favorably of them,
and made conciliatory overtures, and [the
Jews] returned to their country and birthplace as before [1: 139].

[4]   5303 [1543]. R. Abraham of Prague was
eminent in Torah study. He composed
a supercommentary on Rashi of blessed
memory, and impressive glosses on the *Tur
Oraḥ Ḥayyim*. He taught many disciples
and was expert in the seven sciences. He
was the head of the yeshivah and president
of the rabbinical court here in the holy
community of Prague. He ascended to
God in 5303 as I saw written on his
tombstone [1: 139].

**Rashi**  Rashi's commentary on the Bible. —TRANS.
***Tur Oraḥ Ḥayyim***  one part of the four-part legal work composed by R. Jacob b. Asher that deals with blessings, prayers, the Sabbath, festivals, and fasts. —TRANS.

---

3.  See Historical Notes, *Chronicle,* no. 51, and the introduction.
4.  The reference is to R. Abraham b. Avigdor. See O. Muneles, "Die Rabbiner der Altneuschul," *Judaica Bohemiae* 5 (1969): 99–100.

[5]   5319 [1559]. All the holy books in our holy
      community, Prague, were confiscated by
      royal permit, in consequence of a false ac-
      cusation that we prayed for the [non-Jews']
      harm. For this reason all the prayer books,
      along with the remaining books, weighing
      eighty talents, were sent to Vienna; there-
      fore, even the *ḥazzanim* had to pray from
      memory in the synagogue, until it became
      clear and was made known to the king that
      the accusation was entirely false. All the
      books were returned. This occurred in the
      year 5319 [1: 141].

[6]   At that time there was a fire in the Ju-
      denstraße and seventy-two houses were
      burned on the 17th of Tammuz [22 June].

      In that year, 5319 [1559], wrath came forth
      from Emperor Ferdinand of blessed mem-
      ory against all the Jews here in Prague. [He
      issued] a royal edict expelling all the Jews
      from his kingdom. Not a single Jew re-
      mained in the entire kingdom of Bohemia.
      In Prague, only twelve [Jewish] house-
      holders were allowed to remain somewhat
      longer. But it was not long before the king
      was overcome with [sympathetic] feelings
      for the Jews and he pardoned them, and
      made conciliatory overtures. [The Jews]
      returned to their land and possessions as
      before, living there securely to this day
      [1: 141].

---

5. See Historical Notes, *Chronicle,* no. 54, and the introduction.
6. See Historical Notes, *Chronicle,* no. 53, and the introduction.

[7]                              Gloss
Thus notes the printer, R. Solomon b.
Mordecai Katz of blessed memory, known
as Mordecai Zemah. The successful intercession and great salvation wrought by my
father of blessed memory in connection
with the expulsion is well known. He
headed the deputation of *shtadlanim* that
appealed to the emperor, dukes, and lords.
Taking his life in his hands, he travelled
through Italy to Rome, returning with
beneficial letters from the pope to the emperor releasing him from his vow. By divine grace, the words of the pope bore
fruit. The emperor obeyed him, and was
overcome with [sympathetic] feelings for
us, for he was a merciful king, and treated
us benevolently. This matter could be
greatly amplified, but I do not want to
comment at length. End of gloss [1: 141].

[8]   5334 [1574]. It was a time of trouble for
Moravian Jewry, when several Jews were
burned in sanctification of the Name. Then
Emperor Maximilian of blessed memory
was kind to them, and we were saved by
virtue of his mercy and righteousness
[1: 143].

[9]   5343 [1583]. R. Isaac Melnik, teacher of the
Torah, head of the yeshivot, and president
of the rabbinical court in the holy commu-

---

7. On the printer's father, R. Mordecai b. Gershom ha-Kohen, founder of the Hebrew
   press in Prague, see O. Muneles, *Epitaphs from the Ancient Jewish Cemetery of
   Prague* (Hebrew; Jerusalem, 1988), 260–62.
8. We have no knowledge of any other documentation for the tragic events of 1574 in
   Moravia.
9. Other members of R. Isaac Melnik's family are mentioned in official documents of the
   Prague town council. See Muneles, "Die Rabbiner der Altneuschul," 100–101;
   idem, *Epitaphs,* 232–33.

nity of Prague for thirty years, died in 5343, leaving behind a blessing to fill his place—his son, R. Ḥayyim, may God protect and preserve him. R. Ḥayyim taught Torah, and was the head of the yeshivah and president of rabbinical court in the holy community of Austerlitz, where he raised many disciples. At present, with the conclusion of [the writing of] this book, he resides with us and is one of our city's most prominent *dayyanim* [judges] [1: 143].

[10]  5344 [1584]. R. Isaac Chajjut, the great rabbi renowned throughout the Diaspora for his teaching and his many disciples, author of *Sefer Paḥad Yitzhak, Siaḥ Yitzhak, Sefer Pney Yitzhak,* and the major work *Kiryat Arba,* and many additional treatises, came here, to Prague, in 5344. He was head of the yeshivah and president of the rabbinical court for three and a half years. May God grant him a long and pleasant life, and may he be exalted [1: 143].

[11]  5352 [1592]. In his benevolence, our master, the renowned luminary Emperor Rudolf, may he be exalted, sent for our teacher R. Loew b. Bezalel, gretting him graciously, and speaking with him face to face as one man speaks to another [Exod. 33:11]. Their conversation dealt with esoteric subjects. This took place here, in Prague, on Sunday, the 3rd of Adar [16 February 1592].

10. R. Isaac b. Abraham Chajjut was the MaHaRaL's brother-in-law. See Muneles, "Die Rabbiner der Altneuschul," 103; J. Elbaum, *Openness and Insularity* (Hebrew; Jerusalem, 1990), 23, 128–30.
11. The meeting between R. Loew (the MaHaRaL) and Emperor Rudolf II in Prague is compatible with various traditions regarding Rudolf's interest in Jewish mysticism. See Evans, *Rudolf II and His World,* 239–42.

The great rabbi R. Loew, scion of sages, is outstanding in our generation. Nations walk in his light, and his wisdom inspires the Diaspora. He is the author of *Sefer Gur Aryeh,* a supercommentary on Rashi of blessed memory, *Sefer Gevurot ha-Shem,* and *Sefer Derekh Ḥayyim,* a commentary on [the Mishnaic tractate] *Avot,* as well as many other works whose illumination we have not yet been worthy of receiving. He was head of the yeshivah and president of the rabbinical court for all of Moravia for twenty years. Then he came here, to Prague, in 5333 [1573], raising many disciples, and founding a meeting place for the Sages [Avot 1:4], the large *bet midrash* which is called the Klaus. He taught Torah there for eleven years, and at a later date, for an additional four years. On Thursday, the 4th of Iyyar 5352 [16 April 1592], he set out for the holy community of Posen, where he was appointed head of the yeshivah, and again assumed the post of president of the rabbinical court for the entire district of Great Poland. May God grant him a long life. May we see the King in His glory; He will rule the world justly. [Isa. 33:17; Ps. 98:9] [1: 145–46].

[12] The great rabbi R. Mordecai Jaffe, eminent in wisdom and years, bearer of the banner of Israel, is the author of the outstanding treatise *Sefer Levush Malkhut* containing all

---

12. R. Mordecai Jaffe was one of the leading Jewish scholars in Prague during the latter half of the sixteenth century. See L. Kaplan, "Rabbi Mordekhai Jaffe and the Evolution of Jewish Culture in the Sixteenth Century" in *Jewish Thought in the Sixteenth Century,* ed. B. D. Cooperman (Cambridge, Mass., 1983), 266–82.

the rulings of the Talmud and the *posekim*.
He composed a book of sermons and com-
mentaries on the Pentateuch, on Mai-
monides' *Guide to the Perplexed* and *Laws of
Sanctification of the New Moon,* as well as a
supercommentary on [R. Menaḥem b.
Benjamin] Recanati['s *Commentary on the
Pentateuch*]. For a long time, some twenty
years, he served as head of the yeshivah and
president of the rabbinical court in the
holy communities of Grodno, Lublin, and
Kremnitz, teaching many disciples. He
was the greatest of the heads of the yeshivot and *dayyanim* [judges] of the "three
lands" [a division of Poland]. He arrived
here in Iyyar 5352 [April/May 1592] and still
dwells in Prague. May he be exalted
[1: 146].

[13]    The great deeds of R. Mordecai Meisel—
pillar of the *bet midrash,* foremost philanthropist and father of the poor, who
sought the good of his people and was
popular with his brethren [Esther 10:3],
the great provider—deserve to be recorded. I feel impelled to mention some of
his works at the conclusion of this book,
that they may be remembered in every city,
in every generation, and in every family.
For his memory will never perish because
of the righteous deeds he performed for us
here in the holy community of Prague. He
built the Hochschul from his own money.
He also donated several Torah scrolls with
artistically wrought gold and silver orna-

---

13.  On R. Mordecai Meisel and his family, see Muneles, *Epitaphs,* 265–68; Evans, *Rudolf
II and His World,* 240–41.

ments to our community, as well as to other communities in Poland, and the holy city Jerusalem. He also built the public bathhouse and the ritual bath, the poorhouse for the indigent, and paved the Judenstraße with stone flagstones, all at his own expense. In addition to all these, he built an exceedingly splendid great synagogue, unmatched in beauty in the entire Diaspora, erecting it on twenty columns of hewn stone. At present, as I near the end of my book, the work has been completed. The overseers, including skilled masons like Mr. Joseph Wahl and Hertz Zoref, estimate that its construction cost more than ten thousand thalers [1: 146].

# Glossary

*bet din:* a rabbinic court of law.

*bet midrash:* school for higher rabbinic learning, often attached to a synagogue.

*dayyan:* a rabbi qualified to serve as a judge on a rabbinic court.

*halakhah:* the legal side of Judaism that embraces personal, social, national, and international relationships, as well as the practices and observances of Judaism.

*Ḥanukkah:* the eight-day celebration commemorating the victory of Judah Maccabee over the Syrian king Antiochus Epiphanes and the subsequent rededication of the Temple.

*ḥazzan(im):* the cantor or prayer leader who officiates in the synagogue. In medieval times the ḥazzan was a salaried synagogue official.

*Hoshana Rabbah:* the seventh day of the festival of Sukkot observed on the 21st of Tishri and marked by special prayers and observances.

*Isru Ḥag:* designation for the day following the three pilgrim festivals; often treated as a sort of minor holiday.

*Judenstraße:* Jewish quarter.

*kehillah:* the organized Jewish community of a city, overseeing the administration of charities and communal affairs.

*minyan(im):* group of ten adult male Jews, the minimum necessary for communal prayer.

*Ninth of Av (Tisha be-Av):* a Jewish fast-day observed on the 9th day of Av in commemoration of the destruction of the First and Second Temples.

*pinkas:* community register or minutes book. In the Middle Ages each community, and various local societies such as artisan guilds, had its own *pinkas* in which were recorded minutes of meetings, by-laws, lists of elected officials, unusual events, and so forth.

*posek(im):* decider; codifier or rabbinic scholar who pronounces decisions on questions of Jewish law.

*Rosh Ḥodesh:*   new moon, marking the beginning of the month in the Jewish calendar.

*Shavuot:*   Pentecost; Feast of Weeks. Second of the three annual pilgrim festivals, commemorating the receiving of the Torah at Mt. Sinai.

*Shemini Azeret:*   a one-day (two-day in the Diaspora) holiday celebrated at the conclusion of Sukkot.

*shetar(ot):*   formal legal document or deed which requires the signatures of witnesses.

*shtadlan(im):*   court Jew; a representative of Jewish interests with access to dignitaries of state, or active at royal courts. The *shtadlan's* intervention was most frequently occasioned by taxation, blood libel and Host desecration accusations, as is well demonstrated by the activities of the famous court Jew, R. Joseph of Rosheim.

*Simḥat Torah:*   Rejoicing of the Torah. Holiday marking the completion in the synagogue of the annual cycle of reading the Pentateuch, observed in the Diaspora on the day following *Shemini Azeret.*

*Sukkot:*   Feast of Booths (or Tabernacles). Last of the three pilgrim festivals, beginning on the 15th of Tishri.

*takkanot:*   regulations supplementing the Law of the Torah; regulations governing the internal life of communities and congregations.

*yeshivah:*   Traditional Jewish academy primarily devoted to the study of rabbinic literature.

*yizkor:*   a Jewish memorial prayer for the dead usually recited in the synagogue on Yom Kippur, on *Shemini Azeret,* on the last day of Passover, or on Shavuot.

*Yom Kippur:*   Day of Atonement; a solemn fast day falling on the 10th of Tishri and marked by continuous prayer and repentance.

# Bibliography

## Primary Sources

Abraham Zacuto. *Sefer ha-Yuhasin ha-Shalem*. Edited by Z. H. Filipowski with an introduction by A. H. Freimann. Jerusalem, 1963.

Bondy, G., and F. Dworsky, comps. *Zur Geschichte der Juden in Böhmen, Mähren und Schlesien*. 2 vols. Prague, 1906.

David Gans. *Sefer Zemah David*. Edited by M. Breuer. Jerusalem, 1983.

David ha-Reuveni. *Sippur*. Edited by A. Z. Aescoly. Jerusalem, 1940.

Davidson, I. *Oṣar ha-Shirah ve-ha-Piyyut*. New York, 1924.

"Élie Capsali et sa Chronique de Venise." *REJ* 79 (1924): 28–60.

Elijah b. Asher Ashkenazi (Bahur). *Masoret ha-Masoret*. Venice, 1538.

Elijah Capsali. *Seder Eliyahu Zuta*. 2 vols. Machon Ben Zvi and Tel Aviv University, 1976–1977.

Gedaliah ibn Yahya. *Shalshelet ha-Kabbalah*. Venice, 1587.

*Gezerot Ashkenaz ve-Ṣorfat*. 2d ed. Edited by A. M. Habermann. Jerusalem, 1971.

*Iggerot Erez Yisrael*. 2d ed. Edited by A. Yaari. Ramat Gan, 1971.

Jacob b. Eliezer Ulma. *Qinah al Gerush Sefarad*. In *Min Hagenazim*, edited by Y. L. Bialer. Jerusalem, 1967.

Joseph ha-Kohen. *Divrey ha-Yamim le-malkhey Ṣorfat u-malkhey beyt Ottoman ha-Tugar*. 2 vols. Sabbioneta, 1554. Vol. 3. Edited by D. A. Gross. Jerusalem, 1955.

———. *Emeq ha-Bakha*. Edited by K. Almbladh. Uppsala, 1981.

———. *The Vale of Tears*. Translated by H. S. May. The Hague, 1971.

Joseph of Rosheim. "Rabbi Joselmann de Rosheim: Diary" (French). Edited by J. Kracauer. *REJ* 16 (1888): 85–95.

———. *Sefer Hammiknah*. Edited by H. Fränkel-Goldschmidt. Jerusalem, 1970.

Mordecai Jaffe. *Levush Mordecai*. A commentary on the *Shulhan Arukh, Orah Hayyim*. Prague, 1623.

Neubauer, A., and M. Stern. *Hebraeische Berichte über die Judenverfolgungen während der Kreuzzüge*. Vol. 1. Berlin, 1892.

Salfeld, S. *Das Martyrologium des nürnberger Memorbuches*. Berlin, 1898.

Samuel Usque. *A Consolation for the Tribulations of Israel*. Third dialogue. Translated by G. I. Gelbart. New York, 1964.

*Wormser Minhagbuch des R. Jousep (Juspa) Schammes*. Edited by E. Zimmer. Jerusalem, 1988.

## Secondary Sources

Aescoly, A. Z., ed. *Jewish Messianic Movements.* Jerusalem, 1956.

Akawya, A. A. "Qeviat Zemaney sheney ha-Miqdashim ve-Ḥurbanam." *Tarbiz̧* 39 (1970): 349–55.

Altmann, A. *Geschichte der Juden in Stadt und Land Salzburg.* Vol. 1. Berlin, 1913.

Aptowitzer, V. *Mavo le-Sefer Ravyah.* Jerusalem, 1938.

Ashtor, E. *The Jews of Moslem Spain.* Vol 1. Translated by A. Klein and J. M. Klein. Philadelphia, 1973.

Avi-Yonah, M. *The Jews under Roman and Byzantine Rule.* Jerusalem, 1984.

Bamberger, S. *Geschichte der Rabbiner der Stadt und des Bezirkes Würzburg.* Wandsbek, 1905.

Baron, S. W. *A Social and Religious History of the Jews.* Vols. 13–14. Philadelphia, 1969.

Beinart, H. "Cuando Llegaron los Judios a España?" *Estudios* 3 (1961): 1–32.

———. "Shtey Ketovot Shalom al Yisrael mi-Sefarad." *Eretz-Israel* 8 (Sefer Sukenik, 1967): 298–304.

Benayahu, M. *Ha-Yaḥasim she-beyn Yehudey Yavvan le-Yehudey Italyah.* Tel Aviv, 1980.

Ben-Sasson, H. H. "Le-Megamot ha-Khronografiyah ha-Yehudit shel Yemey ha-Beynayyim." *Historyonim ve-Askolot Historiyot,* 29–49. Jerusalem, 1962.

———. "The Reformation in Contemporary Jewish Eyes." *The Israel Academy of Sciences and Humanities, Proceedings* 4 (1970): 239–326.

Bernfeld, S. *Sefer ha-Demaot.* Vol. 2. Berlin, 1924.

Bialloblotsky, C. H. F., trans. *The Chronicles of Rabbi Joseph ben Joshua ben Meir the Sphardi.* London, 1835.

Bibl, V. *Maximilian II der rätselhafte Kaiser, ein Zeitbild.* Leipzig, 1929.

Bosl, K. *Handbuch der Geschichte der böhmischen Länder.* 2 vols. Stuttgart, 1967–1974.

Breuer, M. "R. David Gans, Author of the Chronicle Z̧emaḥ David" (Hebrew), *Bar Ilan* 11 (1973): 97–118.

Brilling, B. "Eine Eingabe der böhmischen Judenheit vom Jahre 1560." *Zeitschrift für die Geschichte der Juden in der Tschechoslowakei* 5 (1938): 59–62.

Brockman, E. *The Two Sieges of Rhodes, 1480–1522.* London, 1969.

Buchholtz, F. B. *Geschichte der Regierung Ferdinand der ersten.* Vol. 3. Vienna, 1832. Vol. 4. Vienna, 1833.

Cahana, I. Z. *Meḥqarim be-Sifrut ha-Teshuvot,* 163–94. Jerusalem, 1973.

Chroust, A. *Von Einfall des Passauer Kriegsvolks bis zum nürnberger Kurfürstentag.* Munich, 1903.

David, A. "Le-Siyumah shel ha-Negidut be-Misrayim u-le-Toldotav shel Avraham di Castro." *Tarbiz̧* 41 (1972): 332–33.

———. "Mifalo ha-historiyografi shel Gedalya ibn Yaḥya Baal *Shalshelet ha-Kabbalah.*" Ph.D. diss., Hebrew University, Jerusalem, 1976.

———. "Iggeret Yerushalmit mi-Reshit ha-Shilton ha-Ottomani be-Ereẓ Yisrael." In *Peraqim be-Toldot Yerushalayim be-Reshit ha-Tequfah ha-Ottomanit,* edited by A. Cohen, 39–60. Jerusalem, 1979.

———. "Le-Qorot Yehudey Italyah be-Ṣilah shel ha-Reyaqsiyah ha-Qatolit be-Meah ha-16 Le-or Teudot Ḥadashot." *Tarbiz* 49 (1980): 366–68.

———, ed. *Shtey Khroniqot Ivriyot mi-Dor Geyrush Sefarad.* Jerusalem, 1979.

Degani, B. Z. "Ha-Mivneh shel ha-Historiyah ha-Olamit u-Geulat Yisrael be-Zemaḥ David le-R. David Gans." *Zion* 45 (1980): 173–200.

Dinur, B. Z. *Yisrael ba-Golah.* Vol. 2, book 2. Jerusalem, 1967.

Donath, L. *Geschichte der Juden in Mecklenburg.* Leipzig, 1874.

Elbaum, J. *Petiḥut ve-Histagrut.* Jerusalem, 1990.

Ettinger, S. "Ha-Hashpaah ha-Yehudit al ha-Tesisah ha-Datit be-Mizraḥah shel Eyropah be-Sof ha-Meah ha-15." *Sefer Yovel le-Yitzhak Baer,* 228–47. Jerusalem, 1960.

Evans, R. J. W. *Rudolf II and His World.* Oxford, 1973.

Fränkel-Goldschmidt, H. *Mavo le-Sefer Hammiknah le-Yosef Ish Rosheim.* Jerusalem, 1970.

Franz, G. *Der deutsche Bauernkrieg.* Darmstadt, 1975.

Friedländer, M. H. *Zur Geschichte der Blutbeschuldigungen gegen die Juden im Mittelalter und der Neuzeit (1171–1882).* Frankfurt am Main, 1883.

*Germania Judaica.* Vol. 1. Frankfurt am Main, 1917. Vol. 3. Tübingen, 1987.

Gottesdiener, A. "Ha-Ari she-be-Ḥakhmey Prag." *Azkkarah le-nishmat ha-Rav . . . Kook, Qoveṣ Torani Madai* 3–4 (1937): 253–430.

Graetz, H. *History of the Jews.* Vol. 4. Philadelphia, 1956.

Gyorgy, S. *A Török hóditók elleni védelem üsye a dózsa Paraszthåborutól Mohacsig.* Budapest, 1952.

Habermann, A. M. *Gezerot Ashkenaz ve-Ṣorfat.* Jerusalem, 1971.

Hacker, J. "Mikhtav Ḥadash al Tesisah Meshiḥit be-Ereẓ Yisrael u-ba-Golah be-Reshit ha-Meah ha-16." *Shalem* 2 (1976): 355–60.

———. "Shitat ha-Sürgün ve-Hashpaatah al ha-Ḥevrah ha-Yehudit be-Imperiyah ha-Otmanit be-Meot ha-15-17." *Zion* 55 (1990): 63–65.

Haenle, S. *Geschichte der Juden im ehomligen Fürstenthum Ansbach.* Ansbach, 1867.

Heise, W. *Die Juden in der Mark Brandenburg bis zum Jahre 1571.* Berlin, 1932.

Herman, J. "The Conflict between Jewish and Non-Jewish Population in Bohemia before the 1541 Banishment." *Judaica Bohemiae* 6 (1970): 39–54.

Herzog, D. *Urkunden und Regesten zur Geschichte der Juden in der Steiermark (1475–1585).* Graz, 1934.

Heymann, F. G. *John Zizka and the Hussite Revolution.* Princeton, 1955.

Hirsch, A. *Handbuch der historisch-geographischen Pathologie.* Vol. 1. Stuttgart, 1881.

Hock, S. *Die Familien Prags, nach den Epitaphien des Alten Jüdischen Friedhofs in Prag.* Pressburg, 1892.

Hook, J. *The Sack of Rome, 1527.* London, 1972.

Horovitz, M. *Frankfurter Rabbinen: Ergänzungen von J. Unna.* Jerusalem, 1969.

Jakobowitz, T. "Die jüdischen Zünfte in Prag." *Jahrbuch der Gesellschaft für Geschichte der Juden in der Cecholovakischen Republik* 8 (1936): 61ff.

Kaldy-Nagy, G. "Contribution to the Jews of Buda in 1526: Banishment or Resettlement?" *Occident and Orient, a Tribute to the Memory of A. Scheiber.* Budapest and Leiden, 1988, pp. 257–60.

Kaplan, L. "Rabbi Mordekhai Jaffe and the Evolution of Jewish Culture in Poland in the Sixteenth Century." *Jewish Thought in the Sixteenth Century,* 266–82. Edited by B. D. Cooperman. Cambridge, Mass., 1983.

Katzburg, N. "Le-Toldot ha-Yehudim be-Ungariyah be-Tequfat ha-Shilton ha-Turki." *Sinai* 31 (1952): 339–42.

Kaufman, J. R. *Yom Tov Lipmann Muelhausen.* New York, 1927.

Kaufmann, D. "Die Märtyrer des pösinger Autodafés von 1529." *MGWJ* 38 (1894): 426–29.

Kisch, G. *The Jews in Medieval Germany.* 2d ed. New York, 1970.

Kleinberger, A. F. *Ha-Maḥshavah ha-Pedagogit shel ha-Maharal mi-Prag.* Jerusalem, 1962.

Kupfer, E. "Ḥezyonotav shel R. Asher b. R. Meir ha-mekhuneh Lemlein Roitlingen." *Kobeẓ Al Yad* 8 (1975): 385–423.

Kurz, F. *Der Einfall des von Kaiser Rudolf II, in Passau angeworbenen Kriegvolks in ober Östrreich und Böhmen (1610–1611).* Linz, 1897.

Léonard, E. G. *A History of Protestantism.* Vol. 1. London, 1965.

Lewin, R. *Luthers Stellung zu den Juden.* Berlin, 1911.

Lhotsky, A. *Das Zeitalter des Hauses Österreich.* Vienna, 1971.

Lieben, K. *Gal-ed.* Prague, 1856.

Lieben, S. H. "Die ramschak Chronik." *Jahrbuch der Gesellschaft für Geschichte der Cechoslovakischen Republik* 1 (1929): 369–409.

Loewenstein, L. "Memorbücher." *ZGJD* 1 (1887): 196–97.

Loewinger, S. "Recherches sur l'oeuvre apologétique d'Abraham Farrissol." *REJ* 105 (1940): 23–52.

Loserth, J. "Die Stände Mährens und die protestantischen Stände Österreichs ob und unter der Enns in der zweiten Hälfte des Jahres 1608." *Zeitschrift des deutschen Vereins für die Geschichte Mährens und Schlesiens* 4 (1900): 226–78.

Marcus, S. "Le-Toldot ha-Yehudim be-Rodos bi-Yemey Shilton Misdar Abirey Yoḥanan ha-Qadosh." *Oẓar Yehudey Sefarad* 2 (1959): 66–68.

Marx, A. "Le faux Messie Ascher Lemlein." *REJ* 61 (1911): 135–38.

Merriman, R. B. *Suleiman the Magnificent.* Cambridge, Mass., 1944.

Mueller, L. *Aus fünf Jahrhunderten.* Augsburg, 1900.

Muenzer, Z. "Die Altneusynagoge in Prag." *Jahrbuch der Gesellschaft für Geschichte der Juden in der Cechoslovakischen Republik* 4 (1932): 63–105.

Muneles, O. *Prague Ghetto in the Renaissance Period.* Prague, 1965.

———. "Die Rabbiner der Altneuschul." *Judaica Bohemiae* 5 (1969): 99–101, 103.

———. *Ketovot mi-Beyt ha-Almin ha-Yehudi ha-Atiq bi-Prag.* Jerusalem, 1988.

Neher, A. *Le puits de l'Exil: La théologie dialectique du Maharal de Prague.* Paris, 1966.

Netanyahu, B. *Don Isaac Abravanel.* Philadelphia, 1972.

*New Catholic Encyclopedia.* 16 vols. New York, 1967.

Newman, L. I. *Jewish Influence on Christian Reform Movements.* New York, 1925.

Pastor, L. *History of the Popes.* Vol. 9. London, 1910.

Polak-Rokycana, J. "Die Geschichte der Juden in Böhmen in den alten böhmischen Jahrbüchern." *Zeitschrift für die Geschichte der Juden in der Tschechoslowakei* 2 (1931): 175–76.

*Proceedings, Eighth World Congress of Jewish Studies.* Vol. 2. Jerusalem, 1982.

Rosanes, S. *Divrey Yemey Yisrael be-Torgarmah.* Part 2. Husiatyn, 1911.

Rosenberg, A. *Beiträge zur Geschichte der Juden in Steiermark.* Leipzig, 1914.

Schnizlein, A. "Zur Geschichte der Vertreibung der Juden aus Rothenburg O. Tauber 1519/20." *MGWJ* 61 (1917): 263–84.

Scholem, G., and M. Beit-Aryeh. *Sefer Meshare Qitrin.* Introduction to the facsimile edition. Jerusalem, 1977.

Schottky, J. M. *Prag wie es war und wie es ist.* 2 vols. Prague, 1830.

Schwarzfuchs, S. "Maaseh be-Kehillat Roma be-Maḥaṣitah ha-Rishonah shel ha-Meah ha-16." In *Scritti in Memoria di Enzo Sereni,* p. 137. Jerusalem, 1970.

Sedinova, I. "Czech History as Reflected in the Historical Work by David Gans." *Judaica Bohemiae* 8 (1972): 74–83.

Shaw, S. *History of the Ottoman Empire and Modern Turkey.* Vol. 1. Cambridge, 1976.

Sheiber, A. "Qedoshey Phising [Pösing]." *Aresheth* 6 (1980): 227–30.

Sokolow, N. *Ha-Asif* 6 (1894): 133. (2nd pagination.)

Sonne, I. *Mi-Paulus ha-Reviʿi ad Pius ha-Ḥamishi.* Jerusalem, 1954.

Spiegel, S. "Mi-Pitgamey ha-Aqeydah. Serufey Blois ve-Hitḥadshut Alilot ha-Dam." In *Sefer Yovel Li-Khvod M. M. Kaplan.* New York, 1953.

Stein, A. *Die Geschichte der Juden in Böhmen.* Brünn, 1904.

Steinherz, S. "Sage und Geschichte." *Jahrbuch der Gesellschaft für Geschichte der Juden in der Cechoslovakischen Republik* 9 (1938): 138ff.

———. "Geyrush ha-Yehudim mi-Boehm be-shnat 1541." *Zion* 15 (1950): 70–92.

———, ed. *Die Juden in Prag: Bilder aus ihrer tausendjährigen Geschichte.* Prague, 1927.

Stern, M. "Achtenstuecke zur Vertreibung der Juden aus Nördlingen." *ZGJD* 4 (1890): 87–91.

———. *Andreas Osianders Schrift über die Blutbeschuldigungen.* Berlin, 1903.

————. "Die Vertreibung der Juden aus Weissenburg 1520." *ZGJD*, n. s., 1 (1929): 297–303.

Stern, M., and S. Salfeld. *Die israelitische Bevölkerung der deutschen Städte*. Vol. 3, *Nürnberg im Mittelalter*. Kiel, 1894–1896.

Stern, S. *Josel von Rosheim*. Stuttgart, 1959.

Strack, H. L. *Der Blutaberglaube in der Menschheit*. Munich, 1892.

Szulwas, M. A. *Die Juden in Würzberg während des Mittelalters*. Berlin, 1934.

Talmage, F. Introduction to *Sefer Hanizzahon le-R. Yom Tov Lipmann Muelhausen*. Jerusalem, 1983.

Tamar, D. "Ha-Ṣipiyah be-Italyah le-shnat ha-Geulah [5]335." *Sefunot* 2 (1958): 61–88.

Tishby, I. *Meshihiyut be-Dor Geyrushey Sefarad u-Portugal*. Jerusalem, 1985.

Toch, M. "Kehillat Nuremberg be-shnat 1489—Mivneh ḥevrati ve-demografi." *Zion* 45 (1980): 60–72.

Turetschek, C. "Die Türkenpolitik Ferdinands I von 1529 bis 1532." Ph.D. diss., Vienna, 1968.

Urbach, E. E. *Baaley ha-Tosafot*. 4th edition. 2 vols. Jerusalem, 1980. 5th edition. Jerusalem, 1986.

Volavaka, V. *Praha*. Prague, 1948.

Volavkova, M. *The Pinkas Synagogue*. Prague, 1955.

von Schwarzenfeld, G. *Charles V, Father of Europe*. London, 1957.

————. *Rudolf II, der saturnsche Kaiser*. Munich, 1961.

Wachstein, B. *Die Inschriften des alten Judenfriedhofes in Wien*. Vol 1. Vienna and Leipzig, 1912.

Weil, G. E. *Elie Lévita*. Leiden, 1963.

Weinberger, L. J. "Qinah Hadashah al Qedoshey Blois le-R. Avraham b. R. Shmuel mi-Speyer." *PAAJR* 44 (1977): 41–47.

Williams, G. H. *The Radical Reformation*. Philadelphia, 1961.

Yerushalmi, H. Y. "Clio and the Jews: Reflections on Jewish Historiography in the Sixteenth Century." *PAAJR (Jubilee Volume)* 46–47 (1979–80): 607–638.

Zfatman-Biller, S. "Geyrush Ruḥot be-Prag be-Meah ha-17, le-Sheelat Mehaymanuto ha-Historit shel Genre Ammami." *Mehqarey Yerushalayim be-Folklor Yehudi* 3 (June 1982): 22–25, 29.

Zimmer, E. *Jewish Synods in Germany during the Late Middle Ages (1286–1603)*, 89–90. New York, 1978.

Zunz, L. *Synagogale Poesie des Mittelalters*. Berlin, 1855.

# Index